MW01680308

BORN FOR DESTINY

Giving Birth to Your Life's Purpose

Written By: Dr. Brian W. Alton
Senior Pastor - Chancellor
Desert Rose Community Church
and Gateway International Bible Institute
Glendale, Arizona

Born For Destiny

Published by:
Intermedia Publishing Group, Inc.
P.O. Box 2825
Peoria, Arizona 85382
www.intermediapub.com

ISBN 978-1-935529-31-6

Printed in the United States of America by Epic Print Solutions

Contents

Dedication

I dedicate this 'first born' book to my family, especially to my wife, Phaedra, who by her testimony experienced both the natural sorrow of bareness and the joy of promised fruitfulness. Without her constant encouragement and support, this book would not have been completed.

To our heritage from the Lord: Brian James, Michael David, Abigail Rose; and Bryanna Lynn, all gifts of love, life, and joy in our lives.

Michael and Abbi: becoming your forever family has filled our hearts with tremendous happiness, and fulfillment.

To my first born son Brian: Your birth mother Alyce would be so proud of the godly man that you have become. Although it was very difficult for her, she was more than courageous in her efforts to give birth to you. Both you and your precious wife Bryanna will have the task of carrying on purpose and destiny in your family and for our future as a family in Christ.

I love you all!

Special Recognition and Acknowledgments

I would like to give special thanks to sister Rheta O'Neal for spending many hours helping me to transcribe all the GIBI "PUSH" teaching CD's for the majority of the content in this book. I wanted to capture the words that the Holy Spirit gave me under the anointing from those incredible sessions I taught throughout the years on this subject. Rheta, you were like a mid-wife who helped me to "PUSH" and give birth to my first born book.

I would also like to once again express my sincere thanks and appreciation to my wife Phaedra for her help in reviewing, formatting, and editing the initial manuscript for "Born For Destiny." This book would not have been a reality without her sacrifice and support. Phaedra you were my birthing coach and encourager. You have a real gift to do this kind of thing and I am so glad because I don't! You are a true helpmate.

To my mom and dad, thank you for your years of support and encouragement. You always taught me to follow my dreams until they became a reality. Thanks for always believing in me, and making me a better person.

A huge "God Bless You" goes out to the Desert Rose Community Church staff, family and the Gateway International Bible Institute faculty and students who encouraged and supported me in the writing of my first book. I want to thank all of you "hearers" and "sitters" in these two families for allowing me to release, teach, and preach this to you over the years. Thank you for your sincere grace and extra patience as I have kept you way over the time allotted me in class and in service. You kept saying 'Amen!" so I just kept right on Pushing!

And lastly, I want to thank my dear Ministry Manager and Personal Assistant Pastor Jerry Masters and Rev. Susi Pennington for doing your best to keep my Pastoral schedule clear from distraction so that I could dedicate my days to finish “Born For Destiny.” I know that many times it added extra work, and longer hours to your own ministry schedules in order to give me the time that I needed in the labor and delivery room to give birth to my own purpose and destiny. You both are true gifts to my Shepherding life.

Foreword

Born for Destiny, written by Dr. Brian Alton, is an insightful journey into the divine design of birthing vision and purpose. I must admit, I have known Brian for quite some time and never dreamed that he would write a book about giving birth, especially from the perspective of a pregnant woman!

I have had the privilege of giving birth to an amazing daughter who has been mightily used of God in a national prayer movement. I believe that she is a product of the creative Word of God, actively pushing her purpose into manifestation. Allow me to explain.

Early on in my pregnancy, I made a decision to have what has been called a "Word Birth." While my child was in my womb, I spoke the Word, prayed the Word, and believed God that my baby's destiny was rooted and grounded in Scripture that creates and sustains kingdom life. Believe me, the Word of God works!

Another reason why this book is special to me is that I am soon to be a grandmother for the first time. I am so excited to see who and what I gave birth to come into fulfilled destiny, by her giving birth to another precious life. I cannot express the joy I am having as I share with my daughter my experience of pouring the Word of truth into her so that she can now do the same to my grandchild.

This is tantamount to the essence of *Born For Destiny*. Dr. Alton shares revelation that has empowered him to PUSH: pray until something happens. This speaks to my passion to have Christians saturated with prayer. In prayer, destinies are birthed. In prayer, purpose is clarified. In prayer, passion is ignited. But, prayer takes work.

Believe me, even though the word was applied in my pregnancy, it took work and a whole lot of pushing to give birth. This is the principle that is in this book. Dr. Alton helps you identify the hindrances, challenges, and seemingly insurmountable odds resisting you fulfilling your destiny. He shares that even through death experiences, God will give you the grace to overcome.

Those who are called and those who are discouraged; those who are depressed and those who think of themselves as forgotten, unloved, or barren, you are "Born for Destiny!"

Cheryl Sacks, co-founder BridgeBuilders International
and author of *The Prayer Saturated Church*

Introduction

Have you ever wondered what you were born for? Why were you created? What is the specific role God has for you to play on this broad highway of humanity? Is there a real reason and meaning to your life? What are you living for? Who are you living for? Are you currently living life to its fullest potential? What kind of legacy will you leave for others after you are gone? Every single human being ever born has asked themselves these kinds of questions at least once. These core questions strike at the heart of all human pursuit. Just like you, all men and women around the world want to know the answers to these vital questions and more.

Were you captivated by the title of this book? Are you hungry and desperate to know your true reason for being? Whether people admit to it or not, finding and fulfilling their true life's purpose and destiny is at the heart of every person's highest ambitions. I believe this book will help. It draws from many powerful passages from the Bible that will help you discover how incredibly significant and important your life and destiny truly is.

The book is designed as a training manual that will give you a step-by-step approach to discovering and fulfilling your true God given purpose and destiny. You will be encouraged throughout these pages to examine your life using a childbirth metaphor. From conception through all the stages of pregnancy, inside and out, your life will be viewed as growing, stretching, and transforming until, at an exact moment in time calculated by heaven's timepiece, the water breaks; then labor and birth. I relate this beautiful processes and experience of giving birth to discovering and fulfilling of one's true life purpose and destiny.

This book is about your passion to understand your life's ultimate meaning and assignment. It's about your search for control over life's many challenges and circumstances and then learning how to overcome them in order to fulfill your ultimate God given destiny. It's about living life to its fullest, and reconnecting you to your true self. It's about where you fit in the grand scheme of things with God the Father, the Creator of the universe.

Nothing happens by accident. There truly is a reason and a meaning for your life. God, by His Spirit, is trying to get your attention. He is trying to satisfy the hunger and the thirsting of your soul. God desires to show you things about your life that you have never seen before. He is trying to reveal to you, by His Spirit, what you couldn't uncover in your own understanding and human reasoning. The contents of this book is a key to help you unlock your own purpose and destiny. It is my prayer that this book will give you a new appreciation for life and will help prepare you to enter a new dimension of divine understanding that will change how you view and respond to the world. Nothing matters more than knowing God's plan and purpose for your life. And nothing can compare to getting in touch with why God created you and why you are here living and breathing at this exact moment in time.

It's time for you to experience a life changing transformation that will help you give birth to your very own unique calling and destiny. You don't have to search aimlessly throughout your life to discover your reason for being any longer; you can uncover the truth of your own purpose and destiny today! The good news is that there is a perfect plan for your life. Each and every one of us has a destiny to fulfill. We were all created and designed by God and born into this world for a very specific reason. The Lord wants you to be able to uncover the many divine clues that will lead you toward the truth of your destiny. From these clues you will be able put the pieces of your purpose together in order one-by-one to discover and live out the unique plan for your life. It's as simple as asking Him to help you solve the mystery and allowing the Holy Spirit to help you put together the many facts and truths to help you solve the clues that will help unravel the mystery and reveal the truth to you. Without a purpose, life is just motion without meaning, activity without direction, and events without reason. Without knowing your purpose, life is trivial, and pointless. The Bible says, "the Spirit gives life" (II Corinthians 3:6). The Lord is just waiting to impregnate you with His purposes and His life! He wants to reveal His plan for your life to help you give birth to New Life in Jesus Christ. He wants you to discover an alternative reality besides the one you are living in now.

Let's pray together before you begin your journey of discovering your purpose and destiny:

Father in the name of Jesus, I desire to know and understand my life's true purpose and destiny - the plan that You have for my life. I realize that this is impossible for me without the help of the Holy Spirit. I ask that you would anoint my eyes and my ears with Your precious Holy Spirit. Open the eyes of my heart to see, open my spiritual ears to hear, and open up and make fertile the spiritual womb of my life that I might become impregnated with the truth - The Divine Seed of Heaven – Jesus Christ. Help me to know how to better understand what You are saying to me about my purpose and destiny. As I read let me hear Your voice within the words of this book. Transform me, impregnate me in the spiritual womb of my life with your purposes and destiny, cause me to become spiritually fertile so that I can become fruitful in my spiritual walk with you. I pray that You bring me from a place of not knowing to a place of knowing my full potential in Your great master plan. Change and transform my life so that I will never be the same again! In the Mighty name of Jesus I pray.

Amen!

Chapter 1
What Are You Searching For?

"For You formed my inward parts; You covered me in my mother's womb. I will praise You, for I am fearfully and wonderfully made; marvelous are Your works, and that my soul knows very well. My frame was not hidden from You, when I was made in secret, and skillfully wrought in the lowest parts of the earth. Your eyes saw my substance, being yet unformed. And in Your book they all were written, the days fashioned for me, when as yet there were none of them..."

Psalms 139:13-16

Have you ever wondered why you were born? Have you ever asked these questions: "Who am I?" "Why am I here?" "Why was I created?" "What is the purpose for my life?" Every single human being ever born on planet earth has asked themselves these questions at least once in their lifetime. It is an unfortunate truth but many people live with a quiet desperation and some actually die plagued by the vague uneasiness that somehow they have "missed it." Others wonder aimlessly, attempting to solve the great purpose and destiny puzzle posed by life. The greatest tragedy in life is not death, but life without a reason for living. It is pointless and depressive to be alive and not know why you were born and given life.

There are over 6 billion people on planet earth and only a small number of them really know why they exist. What a great tragedy! Who is man? Why was he created? Why was he put here on earth? Why was he born? What is he suppose to be doing? Where did he come from? Where is he going? What is his true purpose and destiny for being? These questions strike at the heart of all human pursuit. Men and women around the globe want to know the answers to these all-important questions. The deepest craving of the human spirit is to find a sense of significance and relevance in this life. Do you know yours? If you don't, you can! The search for true meaning is the ultimate pursuit of man. Every culture and every race no matter how old or far removed has developed some form of practice (religious or otherwise) that attempts to answer these questions and to satisfy the vacuum and void in the pit of the human soul.

We all have cried out for reason, purpose, and significance from one generation to the next. For mankind, life on planet earth has been nothing more than a long strenuous and tedious march down the road of time, with each generation searching for something they cannot define in their own human reasoning. From the secret writings and pictures etched on the walls of ancient caves and caverns, to the grand archaeological monuments discovered around the world, to the remains of great empires and underground ruins, man marches on seeking to find himself and to make sense of his world. From the ancient world of the cave men and native African and Indian tribes through the progressive succession of sophisticated cultures, to the advent of the industrial revolution leading to the scientific age of post-modernism and the computer age, we are still no better off nor any different from our great ancestors of old. With every race, culture, socio-economic class, religious and political group under heaven in each one of these societies the search is all the same. We are all on the same journey looking and searching for the same things. From generation to generation we have one thing in common with each other, and that's that we all want to know why we were born and why we were put here on this planet. Simply put, people are and looking for the same answers to the very same questions in life.

These questions are universal; they lurk deep within the secret chambers of every human being regardless of their race, color, and ethnic heritage. In essence, the question is this: "what is the true purpose and destiny for my life?" What makes us all different and sets us apart from each other is the road and systems we implement and develop to find what we are searching for. We know that all religions in the world result from man's search for a 'Supreme Being.' We long to know how we fit into that equation; about our relationship with, and our significance to, that Supreme Being. Therefore, in a sense, all religion is mans attempt to respond to his desire to find some type of meaningful, and possibly intimate relationship with a Supreme Being as he seeks to find some reasonable meaning to life. This human search for reality is natural and common to all human cultures on the planet, and yes, even the self proclaimed Atheist inherently believes that, at the very least, there is 'someone' or 'some-thing' out there not to believe in. The magnificent wonder of the Word of God and the teaching of Christianity is that God says every person has a unique purpose and calling for their life. Every individual counts in God's Kingdom economy. Every person has a piece of God's plan to transform the world.

I believe that secretly, most people would admit they feel they have been created for some specific assignment. Some find that assignment in life quicker than others, while some are still searching relentlessly. Even people who have never been exposed to Christianity, or any formal religion for that matter, believe there is some reason why they were born. Even in the most primitive of societies in our world we find the expression and desire to seek, find, and understand a 'Supreme Being' or 'Higher Power' as evidenced by their relationship to creation, cultural development, and practices of different forms of religious expression.

You can appreciate this thought a little better if you just think about your own existence for a moment. Think about your own world and your different life experiences, religious or otherwise; think about the way you were raised compared to someone else you know. Think about all the different family traditions and holidays you celebrate, or choose not to celebrate, because of your upbringing or religious or cultural background and compare them to someone else you know who celebrates differently. In my ministerial vocational adventure (and I say adventure because every day in full-time ministry is a grand one) I get to travel the globe often and minister the gospel of Jesus Christ to many different kinds of groups and diverse domestic and foreign cultures. Just one little 14 day trip to an impoverished village in a foreign land like Yangon, Myanmar makes me realize quickly just how different my world is in the United Sates. We are all different and unique in many ways, yet no matter how different and unique we are from one another, we are all still the same when it comes to our desire to know and give birth to our life's true purpose and destiny.

With that said let's get back to the main question at hand; the question we all have in life, the question of the ages… "Do you know why YOU were born?" Can you see a purpose for your own life with all of its ups and downs, its mixture of joys and sorrows? What I like to refer to as 'the good, the bad, and the ugly.' Do you see lasting value in all your efforts, toils, challenges and uncertainties? Approximately three thousand years ago King David, God's celebrated chosen king of Israel considered the apparent insignificance of human beings when compared to the vastness of the universe. As a shepherd boy, he had spent many days and nights outdoors gazing at the star-studded night skies of Israel. It was in those moments of starring into the sky in contemplation of his own purpose and destiny that He would record some of his greatest thoughts.

> "When I consider Your heavens, the work of Your fingers, the moon and the stars, which You have ordained, what is man that You are mindful of him, and the son of man that You visit him?"
>
> Psalm 8:3, 4

David wondered why in the world, in this magnificent and vast whole universe, is God Almighty so concerned with human beings and their future? David realized that when he looked at the larger scope of the vast heavens, that we can appear to be absolutely and totally minute and insignificant. Yet he still perceived that in the plan of the great Creator God, no part of His physical creation even begins to compare with His purposes and destiny for human beings. Understanding that only God can reveal His plan and purpose for creating us, David continued his reflection on the purpose and destiny of mankind in verses 5-8:

> "For You have made him a little lower than the angels, and You have crowned him with glory and honor. You have made him to have dominion over the works of Your hands; You have put all things under his feet, all sheep and oxen, even the beasts of the field, the birds of the air, and the fish of the sea that pass through the paths of the seas."

Although these verses give us tremendous clues about discovering mankind's true purpose and destiny still without first accepting and believing in an Omniscient, Omnipresent, All-Powerful, loving Creator God you cannot fully grasp and comprehend the gravity of these verses as they relate to your own ultimate destiny. So let's first consider the meaning of life if evolution were true and if there were no Creator God who had been involved with mankind. Let's further assume there is no life after death and certainly no possibility of immortality. Life would end in the finality of the grave. There would be no transcendent purpose to give meaning to our lives. Our lives would have no more significance than any animal or tiny insect straining for it's survival until the moment of death. All of the achievements, the many sacrifices, the good and wonderful things men and women do would ultimately be futile efforts in a universe awaiting its own ruin.

Unfortunately, the late astronomer and author Carl Sagan didn't believe in God. Even after the death of his wife of 20 years, he believed he would never see her again. As his own death approached him, he expressed a common human longing mixed with the sad futility of atheism. He said "I would love to believe that when I die I will live again, that some thinking, feeling, remembering part of me will continue on. But, as much as I want to believe that, and despite the ancient and worldwide cultural traditions that assert an afterlife, I know of nothing to suggest that it is more than just wishful thinking" (In the Valley of the Shadow; Parade, March 10, 1996). Those words expressed the ultimate despair and sadness from a hopeless and helpless human soul. That's what ultimately happens when you remove the hope of an afterlife. Your life is empty and devoid of hope, it is without value and without a sense of purpose and destiny. If this is truly the case, then what's the difference between living the selfless life of Mother Teresa or the life of an evil tyrant dictator like Adolph Hitler? If this were the case then everyone's fate would be exactly the same. All the good contributions of people's lives would make no difference to their fate or the fate of the world or universe. This is the reality of a dark, barren, and bleak outlook of those who base their beliefs on atheism, evolution and the assumption that this life is all there is. If God really does exist, our lives will have an eternal significance because our hope is not in death but in eternal life. If God exists, then we have a standard of right and wrong and absolute truth residing in the nature of God Himself. This makes our moral choices in this life profoundly important and historically significant.

When Stephen Hawking wrote his book A Brief History of Time, after explaining his view of the nature of the universe, he concluded: "If we find the answer to that (the answer to the universal question of why man and the universe exist), it would be the ultimate triumph of human reason—for then we would know the mind of God" (Hawking, pg. 175). Friends, the answer to that question will not come from human reason or intelligence but only from the One true and living God who transcends our material universe. If we remove God from the equation, we lose all sense of purpose and destiny for man and the entire universe, and that is a sad, hopeless, dark, and depressive perspective of life.

The meaning of life has been a huge question mark from the beginning of time. It is in our nature to ask such questions as "Why am I here?" "Why was I born?" and "What is the purpose and meaning of life?" The good news is that God does have a purpose for man, but the bad news is that few grasp what it is. Knowing your transcendent purpose, and really believing it, can infuse such incredible hope and meaning into your life. But we can only understand our purpose if we seek answers from the One who created the universe and all life as we know it. If you had the opportunity today, what would you ask God the Father - the Supreme Being of the universe if you could get a direct and immediate answer from Him?

I discovered an interesting poll that was taken in the USA Today newspaper that reported that the number 1 question people would like to ask God is "What's my purpose here?" With all our technology and scientific sophistication, we still haven't answered the fundamental question of what is the purpose and value of all human life. Where would you even start to discover the purpose for your own life? Can you find it in psychological tests or philosophy? Aptitude tests might help you pinpoint your abilities. Personality testing could conceivably help you focus on aspects of who you are, but no matter how good and thorough the evaluations are the social sciences can't even explain why you live. The complexity and the interdependency of the nature around us, the miracle of life itself, reveal a Master Creator, a Life Giver. Would it make sense that a brilliant Life Giver would create intelligent beings without a purpose and destiny? The great question of "What's my purpose here?" can ultimately only be answered by the Creator of all life. Our Western society claims to have its roots in Christianity, yet the last place many people search to discover their purpose in life is in the Bible.

The book of Genesis, (which means in Hebrew 'the beginning, or in a beginning), contained in the first book of the Bible in the very first sentence it says: "In the beginning God created the heavens and the earth." But then the Creator God didn't stop there, He then proceeded to create a unique biological being from the dust of the earth whom He placed there under the heavens called man. Genesis 2:7 states, "And the LORD God formed man of the dust of the ground, and breathed into his nostrils the breath of life; and man became a living being." Does this mean that man is just another animal, different in form but essentially the same as a chimpanzee or other mammal? The theory of evolution tries to lead us to that conclusion, but evolution doesn't explain the obvious differences between humanity and animals. How do we explain the human ability to create music and art, discover and use geometry, develop architecture, or even invent complex forms of communication? When we look to nature for answers, we see that a slug or a spider is driven entirely by instinctive behavior. The more complex the life form, the more it can learn. Yet the behaviors of even the highest forms of animals are primarily instinctive, this isn't true of humanity. The ability to reason and make complex decisions and choose courses of action makes humans infinitely different from any animal or creature on the face of the earth.

Once again, we must turn to the Bible. In the Creation account we see that God created each animal 'according to its kind,' but human beings are in the 'image' and 'likeness' of God (Genesis 1:24-28). Creativity, positive emotions, logic, love, abstract thought, and communication skills, these are all aspects of the mind of the Creator. These are ways in which He has created us in His likeness. Notice what the Bible says in Job 32:8: "But there is a spirit in man, and the breath of the Almighty gives him understanding." One of the biblical prophets, Zechariah, declares that God "forms the spirit of man within him" (Zechariah 12:1). The natural creation of a human being during conception is a very beautiful and miraculous process.

It never ceases to amaze me how a man's seed (sperm cells) can travel through a woman's uterus and reach the target of a fertile egg and in just 9 short months life forms; a beautiful new human being. In the search for your own life's true purpose and destiny, you can discover a 'New Birth' process also; it's called the "Eternal Zoë Life of God." It is the same New Life that Jesus Christ said that He came to earth to give to all of us in abundance. It is a life originating in God the Father, conceived and brought forth through His precious Son Jesus Christ, lived out on earth in our purpose and destiny in Christ and ultimately consummated into eternity in Christ at the end of our lives.

Our greatest example of divine purpose and destiny was reflected in the life of Jesus Christ. Jesus had a purpose to fulfill in His own earthly ministry. He actually proclaimed His purpose statement in the gospel of John when He said, "I have come that they (you and I) may have life, and that they may have it more abundantly" (John 10:10). In reality, this 'Zoë Life of God' is a life older than time itself. I am still personally discovering His 'Abundant Life' more and more each and day. This was the very same 'breath of life' that God breathed into the nostrils of our Adam, the father of mankind in the beginning of all things. When He breathed His breath into Adam's nostrils, God's very essence went into him and that's when the Bible says that Adam became a 'living soul' or a 'living being.' (Genesis 2:7) This is when the Lord spoke the creative Word from heaven and sent forth His divine seed from His mouth (breathed His very essence) into the fertile womb of the dust of the earth and gave birth to man in one day. He fashioned, formed, and gave His Life (Zoë Life) to a living being; a son in His likeness and in His image in the Garden and He named him Adam. He then gave his son a purpose.

> "Then God said, 'Let Us make man in Our image, according to Our likeness; let them have dominion over the fish of the sea, over the birds of the air, and over the cattle, over all the earth and over every creeping thing that creeps on the earth.' So God created man in His own image; in the image of God He created him; male and female He created them. Then God blessed them, and God said to them, 'Be fruitful and multiply; fill the earth and subdue it; have dominion over the fish of the sea, over the birds of the air, and over every living thing that moves on the earth.'" (Genesis 1:26-28)

Mankind and animals are both living 'souls,' and beings. Both are subject to death, the difference is, that man possesses a nonphysical component called a spirit that sets him apart and that imparts individuality, intellect, creativity and personality. The Bible reveals the mystery the scientists cannot solve. We are not only physical and chemical beings but we have a non-biological component, a spirit and a soul that is in a limited way like the mind of our Creator.

There is also another vital and important piece that sets man apart from the rest of Creation, and that is the words 'authority' and 'dominion.' God not only blessed man with His great favor and abundant life but He also gave him divine authority and dominion to rule over all of the rest of His Creation, both on land and sea.

As you can see, Adam was birthed into the earth with a very significant and powerful purpose and destiny. Like Adam, I believe that when I first heard the Word of God spoken through a powerful salvation message and when I accepted Jesus Christ as my personal Lord and Savior, it was at that time His Word was implanted into the rich fertile soil of my soul. He breathed His Zoë breath of life inside the spiritual womb of my life and I got pregnant with His divine purpose and destiny.

When God breathed this New Life into my spirit, my heart and my soul were transformed. Something wonderful and unique took place in the fertile womb of my life. He turned my dark bleak barrenness into fruitfulness, and gave me New Life. He turned my meaningless and insignificance into a meaningful life full of divine purpose and destiny! It was from that place of spiritual conception that my personal calling and assignment was birthed.

Through the years, my calling has often been to help others birthing processes of their destiny, very much like how a midwife does for those in natural childbearing. The Lord has accomplished this through equipping me with apostolic and prophetic preaching, teaching, and spiritual gifts. As part of my own purpose and destiny, I have been given a mandate from the Lord to raise up, train up, equip and send out men and women of character and integrity into all the world to preach the Gospel of the Kingdom for the last day end time harvest of souls.

This is at the core of who I am and what I have been called to do for the time that has been allotted to me by God. I believe that I have been called by God to be like a spiritual OB doctor, to help people during their spiritual pregnancy of giving birth to their divine purpose and destiny, and the recuperative period following delivery. This is the anointing that has been 'breathed' into the nostrils of my life, to help men and women discover their redemptive purposes and to help them give birth to their God given destinies.

Chapter 2
An Incomplete Creation

If there is a Creator God, and human beings are like God in so many astonishing ways, why can't we solve our own problems? Why are human beings capable of writing such inspiring music and also able to commit such terrible crimes against each other? We can perform medical research into the intricate details of the human body, we can create medicines that heal our sick, yet we produce nerve gases and chemical warfare agents that can kill masses of people at one time. We can send powerful computerized rocket ships to explore the far regions of outer space but then send missiles hundreds and thousands of miles away that hit its target with pinpoint accuracy intended to destroy a city. If mankind is made in the image of God who reveals Himself as loving, kind and merciful then why are so many of us filled with hatred, violence and selfishness? The answers lie in understanding that without God's true purpose activated in our lives we are still an incomplete creation.

> The LORD God planted a garden eastward in Eden, and there He put the man whom He had formed. And out of the ground

> the LORD God made every tree grow that is pleasant to the sight and good for food. The tree of life was also in the midst of the garden, and the tree of the knowledge of good and evil. (Genesis 2:8, 9)

The book of Genesis reveals the root causes of humanity's evil deeds. The first humans, Adam and Eve, were given freedom to choose between their Creator's instruction about life and a way called "the knowledge of good and evil." Unfortunately under the deception and beguile of the serpent (the devil) they chose the latter, the knowledge of good and evil.

> "Then the LORD God took the man and put him in the Garden of Eden to tend and keep it. And the LORD God commanded the man, saying, 'Of every tree of the garden you may freely eat; "but of the tree of the knowledge of good and evil you shall not eat, for in the day that you eat of it you shall surely die.'" (Genesis 2:15-17)

God told Adam and Eve that once they partook of the fruit of that particular tree that they would start out on the path of self-destruction and separation from Him. He told them that they would ultimately embark on a path that would lead to death. Evil—is what the Bible calls sin, and sin always brings about death. History is a story of good and evil, of incredible potential and incredible failure, and it is also a story of destruction and death. It seems that humanity's destiny without God's divine providence and intervention is doomed to struggle, suffer and eventually die. Central to Christianities belief system and core values is the belief that Jesus of Nazareth is the Son of the living God who took upon Himself humanity's death penalty. Jesus Christ came as the true Messiah to supply the missing link and the key ingredient to make eternal life possible, but on the night before His crucifixion Jesus told His disciples He would send them another 'Helper':

> "If you love Me, keep My commandments, and I will pray the Father, and He will give you another Helper, that He may abide with you forever, "the Spirit of truth, whom the world cannot receive, because it neither sees Him nor knows Him; but you know Him, for He dwells with you and will be in you. "I will not leave you orphans; I will come to you. "A little while longer and the world will see Me no more, but you will see Me. Because I live, you will live also." (John 14:15-19)

The apostle Paul wrote to Christians in the city of Corinth about the missing ingredient that keeps humanity from solving its own problems:

> ."..but we speak the wisdom of God in a mystery, the hidden wisdom which God ordained before the ages for our glory, which none of the rulers of this age knew; for had they known, they would not have crucified the Lord of glory. But as it is written: 'Eye has not seen, nor ear heard, nor have entered into the heart of man the things which God has prepared for those who love Him.' But God has revealed them to us through His Spirit. For the Spirit searches all things, yes, the deep things of God. For what man knows the things of a man except the spirit of the man which is in him? Even so no one knows the things of God except the Spirit of God. Now we have received, not the spirit of the world, but the Spirit who is from God, that we might know the things that have been freely given to us by God." (I Corinthians 2:7-11)

The 'spirit of man' is what makes us have similarities to God and gives us the ability to have a relationship with Him. Paul shows that to really understand the spiritual nature of God we must also receive the Spirit of God. The Spirit of God is the missing 'Chromosome' or ingredient in humanity; without it, human beings become both good and evil, lacking the wisdom to always see and choose the good, and death is always the natural result. Therefore, the death process must be reversed and a new nature developed within us. Peter writes about this issue and tells us what we must become in order for this process to be reversed.

> ."..His divine power has given to us all things that pertain to life and godliness, through the knowledge of Him who called us by glory and virtue, by which have been given to us exceedingly great and precious promises, that through these you may be "partakers" of "the divine nature," having escaped the corruption that is in the world through lust." (II Peter 1:4)

All humanity's problems from agriculture to economics, education to government, family relationships to individual emotional or behavioral health problems are ultimately spiritual in nature. Real solutions require not just a change within an environment but also a change within people. Our first parents (Adam and Eve) chose to participate in both good and evil. Not just Adam and Eve, but every human being who has ever lived except Jesus Christ, has made the same choices. The result is that every human suffers and dies. Jesus came to pay the death penalty for evil. He also came to make available to us the Spirit of God, the healing, the missing ingredient; the right chromosome if you will, that will change us from a corrupted human nature into a divine nature, and then into His image and likeness. What will YOUR ultimate destiny be? What awaits all those who are willing to be changed by God's Spirit from a corrupted human nature to become partakers of the divine nature? Paul explains it in Romans 8:14-17, "For as many as are led by the Spirit of God, these are sons of God. For you did not receive the spirit of bondage again to fear, but you received the Spirit of adoption by which we cry out, 'Abba, Father.' The Spirit itself bears witness with our spirit that we are children of God, and if children, then heirs—heirs of God and joint heirs with Christ...."

The purpose of humanity is to become the spiritual children of God!

We are not called to live as children of sin whose father is the devil, but to be partakers of the divine nature which can only come by re-birth. When we are birthed into the Spirit of God we then become children of God with a loving Father. To be re-birthed into the Spirit we must be 'born again' as Jesus explained to Nicodemus:

> Jesus answered, "Most assuredly, I say to you, unless one is born of water and the Spirit, he cannot enter the kingdom of God. That which is born of the flesh is flesh, and that which is born of the Spirit is spirit. Do not marvel that I said to you, 'You must be born again.' The wind blows where it wishes, and you hear the sound of it, but cannot tell where it comes from and where it goes. So is everyone who is born of the Spirit."
>
> Nicodemus answered and said to Him, "How can these things be?"
>
> Jesus answered and said to him, "Are you the teacher of Israel, and do not know these things? Most assuredly, I say to you, We speak what We know and testify what We have seen, and you do not receive Our witness. If I have told you earthly things and you do not believe, how will you believe if I tell you heavenly things? No one has ascended to heaven but He who came down from heaven, that is, the Son of Man who is in heaven. And as Moses lifted up the serpent in the wilderness, even so must the Son of Man be lifted up, that whoever believes in Him should not perish but have eternal life. For God so loved the world that He gave His only begotten Son, that whoever believes in Him should not perish but have everlasting life. For God did not send His Son into the world to condemn the world, but that the world through Him might be saved." (John 3:5-17)

The purpose for your life is more than getting a good education at an Ivy League school, securing a good job with benefits, making more money, gaining social status and prestige, or seeking fame and fortune. It is the coupling of the human spirit with the Spirit of the living God that makes it possible to have a new nature, and eventually a resurrection to a new life, as immortal children of God, joint heirs with Jesus. This is the ultimate potential of every human being.

The same is true with the new birth experience. When we open up our hearts, accept and receive the Divine Seed of Heaven, Jesus Christ into our lives, He comes into our hearts and plants His loving seed of forgiveness and salvation and we become impregnated with His divine purposes and nature and we are changed, we become "born again" of the spirit of God. We are no longer children of sin and death, but we become children of the living God, birthed and born into a heavenly family, the family of God! This isn't just a nebulous promise of something in the far off future. Our Creator tells us that we can enjoy a Father - child relationship with Him right here and now. There are real solutions to your problems. There is hope for those willing to discover their true purpose and destiny in Him. The first step on that road of discovery is to turn to the Creator. He created you and only He knows how you work, so turn to the owner's manual, the Bible to see the instructions of your design for your future and destiny.

We Are Born Corruptible and Mortal

Before we can truly comprehend our eternal purpose and destiny, we need to clearly understand what man is now. We are all physical beings composed of chemicals and mineral substances from the earth, and that is how God created us.

"And the LORD God formed man of the dust of the ground,

> and breathed into his nostrils the breath of life; and man became a living being." (Genesis 2:7)

Almost all ancient religions have taught error. They have taught us that man has a dual composition, that a human being is both a 'physical body' and an 'immortal soul.' Even today in many parts of the world people believe that after our physical body dies that our supposedly 'immortal soul' will continue on as a living conscious entity apart from the body whether that be in the afterlife somewhere, or in a place called Paradise, in heaven. Some believe we will be re-birthed repeatedly through reincarnation as some other life form that returns back to earth. The idea that we have a soul that is immortal is never taught in the Word of God. In fact, it came to us from the many superstitions of ancient religions, possibly as far back as the Garden of Eden, when Satan convinced Eve she would not die if she disobeyed God's instructions.

> And the woman said to the serpent, "We may eat the fruit of the trees of the garden; but of the fruit of the tree which is in the midst of the garden, God has said, 'You shall not eat it, nor shall you touch it, lest you die.'"

> Then the serpent said to the woman, "You will not surely die. For God knows that in the day you eat of it your eyes will be opened, and you will be like God, knowing good and evil."

> So when the woman saw that the tree was good for food, that it was pleasant to the eyes, and a tree desirable to make one wise, she took of its fruit and ate. She also gave to her husband with her, and he ate. Then the eyes of both of them were opened, and they knew that they were naked.... (Gen-

esis 3:2-7)

> Man is not an immortal being. On the contrary, the Bible clearly tells us that our 'soul' is mortal rather than immortal because it is subject to death. The Bible makes it very clear that immortality is not something we already possess. The Apostle Paul clearly tells us in I Timothy 6:13-16 that God alone is immortal, "I urge you in the sight of God who gives life to all things, and before Christ Jesus who witnessed the good confession before Pontius Pilate, that you keep this commandment without spot, blameless until our Lord Jesus Christ's appearing, which He will manifest in His own time, He who is the blessed and only Potentate, the King of kings and Lord of lords, who alone has immortality, dwelling in unapproachable light, whom no man has seen or can see, to whom be honor and everlasting power. Amen."

Paul even explains in further detail in I Corinthians 15:51-53 that we are 'corruptible' and 'mortal' and 'this mortal must put on immortality' by being changed from corruptible to incorruptible when Jesus Christ returns at the last trumpet. (Also see I Thessalonians 4:16; Revelation 11:15)

> "Behold, I tell you a mystery: We shall not all sleep, but we shall all be changed – in a moment, in the twinkling of an eye, at the last trumpet. For the trumpet will sound, and the dead will be raised incorruptible, and we shall be changed. For this corruptible must put on incorruption, and this mortal must put on immortality. So when this corruptible has put on incorruption, and this mortal has put on immortality, then shall be brought to pass the saying that is written: 'Death is swallowed up in victory.' O Death, where is your sting? O Hades, where is your victory?" (I Corinthians 15:51-55)

At this present time, God's servants are those who "seek for glory and honor and immortality." (Romans 2:7) They do not already possess immortality, but they do understand that Jesus Christ, by sacrificing His life for ours, "...has abolished death and brought life and immortality to light through the gospel." (II Timothy 1:10) Immortality is available only through mankind's Savior, Jesus Christ.

What then is man? Man is mortal! Human life is temporary! We are physical beings who can die; we will all cease to exist. Our life does not reside in some supposed immortal soul. No such teaching can be found in the Holy Scriptures. When we die, our consciousness ceases to exist, it doesn't continue in some other form of energy or creature as portrayed by reincarnation. Our only hope for eternal life lies in the gracious mercy of a loving God.

> "For the wages of sin is death (not immortal life in some other form or place), but the gift of God is eternal life in Christ Jesus our Lord." (Romans 6:23)

Eternal life is the precious gift God has in store for those who turn away from their sin and obey Him. The Bible tells us "He desires all men to be saved and to come to the knowledge of the truth" (I Timothy 2:4). The Bible also tells us that "He is not willing that any should perish but that all should come to repentance" (II Peter 3:9). God desires to give us the precious gift of life forevermore. After we receive this gift of salvation and eternal life in Jesus Christ, God will then do everything He can to ensure that we will come to know our eternal purpose and destiny and fulfill everything He has planned for us.

This truth is beautifully reflected in how a fetus grows and develops inside its mother's womb. During the developmental stages, the fetus fully depends on the placenta to grow and to sustain life. The umbilical cord attaches to the fetus at the navel and there is an immediate metabolic exchange. Nutrients and oxygen in the mother's blood pass through the placenta to the fetus, and metabolic wastes and carbon dioxide from the fetus cross in the other direction; the two blood supplies do not mix. Life cannot be sustained apart from the placenta and the umbilical cord. Without these two organs supplying the proper life-giving elements to the fetus, it would surly die. It's only when the baby has fully developed and has come full term within the pregnancy that it can go from within the womb to be introduced outside of the womb, into the world. As in the natural, so it is in the spiritual realm. Apart from salvation through Jesus Christ, we cannot go from this world to the next. Just as in the glorious example of physical conception and birth our spiritual life cannot be sustained without a divine placenta, which is His precious blood feeding us and becoming a covering over our lives which expels the waste of sin and death and the divine umbilical cord. His dear Son Jesus Christ who feeds us, sustains us, and keeps us whole and healthy until we die and it's time to be introduced to the next dimension, eternal life in Jesus Christ!

Chapter 3
Birthed to Take Dominion

David, the shepherd boy destined to become King of Israel realized that humans are potentially the very best of all of God's creation. He points out that God has already granted humans the supreme capacity to manage the biggest part of His creation on planet earth along with all of its glorious wonders. David concluded that God's purpose for creating humankind, for making us so unique among His creatures, is of the utmost importance in His grand master plan.

In all of God's physical creation, only man was created in the image and likeness of Himself. He gave only man dominion to rule over His creation as well as all the creatures. So mankind is totally unique and was birthed within the creation of God to have dominion. Are you able to grasp what God has in store for those who develop a proper relationship with Him? The Scriptures reveal that our purpose and destiny in this life can go way beyond anything that we could possibly think or imagine. From the very beginning of time, the Lord has had the very best in mind for your life. God's Spirit and His power can empower you to truly discover your purpose and destiny. Only God can do that. He did it in my life and He can do it in your life as well. My own personal life of faith was a response to God's power, not to some fancy verbal, mental, or emotional handiwork made up by man. Just as the Apostle Paul declared by the Spirit of God to God's people in his day and era, I also declare to all of His people in this generation, that what God has already prepared for your purpose and destiny will go way beyond your wildest dreams and imagination! As you seek Him with all of your heart, mind, soul, and strength you, like the countless thousands of other men and women throughout the generations of time have sought after Him will discover your true life's purpose and destiny.

When a person becomes impregnated with divine truth, they conceive and give birth to their purpose and destiny. When that happens, they begin to have plenty of wisdom to pass onto others because truth keeps ones feet firmly planted on solid ground. But the wisdom you receive from God is not the popular wisdom of this world, the fashionable secular wisdom of high-priced experts that will be out-of-date in a few years. I'm not trying to pass on this kind of earthy wisdom to you because the truth is that the wisdom of man will fade away with the years. God's wisdom is eternal and has stood throughout the ages. God's wisdom is something mysterious that goes way down deep into the interior of His plan and purposes for our lives. His is the kind of wisdom that you wouldn't find lying around on the surface of men's minds and thoughts. God's ways and His thoughts are higher than man's ways and his thoughts.

> "For My thoughts are not your thoughts, nor are your ways My ways," says the LORD. "For as the heavens are higher than the earth, so are My ways higher than your ways, and My thoughts than your thoughts. For as the rain comes down, and the snow from heaven, and do not return there, but water the earth, and make it bring forth and bud, that it

> may give seed to the sower and bread to the eater, So shall My word be that goes forth from My mouth; it shall not return to Me void, but it shall accomplish what I please, and it shall prosper in the thing for which I sent it." (Isaiah 55:8-11)

Here we see the prophet Isaiah sharing about the power of God's unfathomable wisdom. He says that He doesn't even think the way you and I think. The way He works isn't the way you and I work. God decrees something so wonderful about Himself here that, as the sky and the stars in the galaxies soar high above the earth, so too His wisdom and works surpass all of man's wisdom and works. Further, the way He thinks is far beyond the way mankind can even begin to think. His wisdom, truth, counsel, and His purposes are like the refreshing rains and snow that descend from the skies and don't precipitate back to the heavens until they've watered the earth. The water does the work of making things grow and blossom, producing seed for the crops of the farmers who supply food. So in like manner, the words of wisdom that come from His mouth do not come back to us empty handed, but they are filled with absolute truth, purpose and destiny. They will do the work that He sent them to do. In other words, they will complete the assignment that He gave them to do.

Do you want to give birth to and complete your divine assignment that you have been given by God to do in your life before you die? Of course you do! Otherwise, you wouldn't be spending your valuable time reading this book right now. We cannot fully complete our assignment in this life without His life and wisdom flowing through us and operating in us. He is the only One who can ultimately help us to complete our heavenly assignment while we still have life and breath. His wisdom is the force and power behind our intended success. Those of us who seek after God's wisdom and not man's will have His life, wisdom, truth, might, and His power operating in us, upon us and through us in all they say and do. He is the propulsion and the force that pushes us forward throughout our life to know and to fulfill our life's true purpose and destiny. What I'm trying to say is not the latest fad, nor the latest popular message, but more like the oldest. God pre-determined the way to bring about His best plan in all of us long before we ever arrived on the scene. Even with all the latest technological discoveries we now have at our fingertips we still haven't a clue about this eternal plan. Once again, God laid it out in plain sight for all of us to see and know that He does have an eternal plan for all of us and that plan goes beyond our wildest dreams.

> "Eye has not seen, nor ear heard, nor have entered into the heart of man the things which God has prepared for those who love Him." (I Corinthians 2:9)

What a glorious Scripture passage! No one in the world has ever seen or heard of anything like this before, never so much as imagined anything quite like it before. What God has purposed and planned for those who love Him and desire to know their purpose, and destiny in His predetermined plan. Isn't it time we let God in all His wisdom explain from His Word what He has in store for us and stop letting others tell us what God can or cannot do? Isn't it time that we stop letting others or even our past circumstances dictate to us who we are and tell us what He can or can't do through us? I say YES IT IS! I say it's time to allow the Divine Seed of Heaven - Jesus Christ the Lamb of God to come into our hearts and into our lives and allow Him through the Spirit of God to impregnate us with His forgiveness and power which will then create within us and birth forth from us our true life's purpose and destiny!

The Search For Significance

Man's lifelong search for significance obviously implies that he is lost without a true knowledge and understanding of his purpose and destiny. It also seems to imply that man's 'need to search' means that something has been lost, that he is lost without the truth and reason for his existence. Therefore, it is not man's choice, rather, it is a burning necessity inside of him to discover the true meaning of his life.

I believe that the best way to find what is missing and what you are searching for in life is to identify what your greatest need and desire is. To understand the divine character and nature of God you have to look at both natural things and spiritual things because the natural speaks of the spiritual, and the spiritual speaks of the natural. For example, natural hunger implies that your body has a need for food; thirst implies that your body has a need for water; loneliness implies that you have a need for companionship. So, we can identify what we lack by what we naturally desire and have need for. The same is true in the spiritual dimension. Spiritual hunger implies that your spirit has a need for spiritual food – the Word of God; spiritual thirst implies that your spirit and soul is thirsting for the life-giving refreshing living water of the Holy Spirit. The good news is that weather it's a natural hunger or thirst or a spiritual hunger or thirst, God can meet each need to the fullest!

Matthew 5:6 says, "Blessed are those who hunger and thirst for righteousness, for they shall be filled."

In His Sermon on the Mount, Jesus was addressing the very same dilemma in the people of His generation. Jesus used man's natural needs like food and water to speak to man's greatest need: his spiritual need. He not only addressed those needs, but He also gave the key for complete happiness, contentment, and fulfillment when He said to them:

> "I am the bread of life. He who comes to Me shall never hunger, and he who believes in Me shall never thirst." (John 6:35)

The Lord wants to satisfy your deepest hunger and thirst. He wants to fill the longing of your soul; He wants to make your dreams a reality. He wants you to be fruitful and multiply in this life. He wants to spiritually impregnate you with something so magnificent that only He could begin to help you think about giving birth to it. He wants to do something so wonderful in and through you in the earth that only He will be able to get all the glory for it when it is finally birthed and made a reality in your life. In the Gospel of John, the Bible declares this remarkable truth about your life and mine: Jesus said, "You did not choose Me, but I chose you and appointed you that you should go and bear fruit, and that your fruit should remain"

This verse declares that God chose you and me first and has predestined and pre-appointed our lives to bare lasting fruit in His Son Jesus Christ. This is the kind of fruit that won't spoil. It is rooted and grounded deep within His love and care for us and in His wonderful plan and purpose for our lives.

Jesus began these passages with the key ingredient for all success in life when He declared boldly in John 15:5, "I am the vine, you are the branches. He who abides in Me, and I in him, bears much fruit; for without Me you can do nothing."

God really does have a remarkable plan and purpose for your life! The Lord is just waiting to reveal it to you. He wants you to mature and grow up in that plan like a healthy fruit filled tree. You and I are the branches of that healthy vine and we are grown up, tethered, supported and grounded solely in God's Son, Jesus Christ, the true vine.

This is similar to how a baby is developed inside a healthy womb of a pregnant expectant mother. The fetus is grown, tethered, and fully supported by the umbilical cord. It's the umbilical cord connecting the embryo or fetus with the placenta of the mother which transports nourishment from the mother to the fetus and discards the wastes from the fetus. The fetus growing inside the womb finds all its nutrients, life source, food, and strength from the umbilical cord or we could say 'the vine' of its mother. It not only provides sustenance and nourishment but it also discards all the waste, or what doesn't belong there. In this light, the umbilical cord is the vine of life and the baby is the branches and it cannot be supported, develop properly, nor be given life without it. Without its mothers 'umbilical vine' it would cease to exist.

The same holds true for the development of our spiritual growth. Our lives apart from Jesus Christ will have no life source. Just like branches on a tree or plant cannot live out their order and purpose apart from the vine. The vine is the root system which supplies the life source that gives life to the whole plant including its branches. Jesus was trying to communicate a powerful truth to us concerning our purpose and destiny through this powerful analogy. He was saying that those who live 'in Me' and stay connected and tethered 'to Me,' and those who build their home 'on Me' will come alive, thrive, and 'survive in Me.' But those who don't will wither up and 'die without Me', and ultimately will die with no sense of purpose and destiny in this life. In the same way that a grape branch cannot bear grapes by itself but only by being joined to the grapevine will it produce a cluster of grapes.

You and I can't bear fruit unless we are joined with Jesus. Jesus said when you're joined 'with Him' and He with you, the relationship becomes intimate, organic and creates a cluster of good throughout your life, and the harvest is sure to be abundant. Separated from Him, we cannot produce a thing. Those who are separated from God become like deadwood, which is only good to be gathered up for a campfire to be burned. Without a purpose, life is motion without meaning, activity without direction, and events without reason. Without knowing your purpose, life is trivial, petty, and pointless.

It doesn't have to be this way, however. In fact, it never was intended to be that way from the beginning. God has always longed to have an intimate close relationship with the best of His creation, mankind. He has always had an important message to bestow upon us. Contained within that message was the sole purpose and reason for our being. Just as God took great pleasure with ordinary men and women long ago, the God of Abraham, Isaac, and Jacob still desires to reveal Himself to you and I today in an extraordinary and personal way. He wants to work out His purposes and promises in and through us in beautiful and fruitful ways that we've never dreamed possible.

Chapter 4
Every Person Has a Unique Calling

> In the Bible God says He wants to show us things that we have never understood or seen before concerning our purpose and destiny; "Thus says the LORD... 'Call to Me, and I will answer you, and show you great and mighty things, which you do not know.'" (Jeremiah 33:2-3)

This passage is declaring that Almighty God, the Creator of all things, all that is seen and unseen, the One true God who made the heavens and the earth, and made it livable and lasting, has a very important message that He wants to bestow upon all of His creation. The message is that if we will call out to Him for answers concerning our life's purpose and destiny, our reason for being, He will answer us and tell us what that reason is. He will show us marvelous and wondrous things about our life that we could never be able to figure out on our own. He can make our life not just livable in the here and now, but He can cause each of our lives to have a lasting impression upon the earth, even beyond our natural years.

Our lives can have true meaning and purpose today, tomorrow, and forever! Isn't that an incredible promise? What is so magnificent about Christianity is the eternal truth that every person has a unique calling and reason for being. Even people who have never met and accepted Jesus Christ as their Lord and Savior believe there has got to be a reason of some kind for why they were born. Yet there are still some people who just don't have a clue as to why they are here and what their purpose in life is.

The good news is that every individual counts in God's economy. Every person has a piece of God's plan to transform their world and sphere of influence. God is trying to get you to understand that there is a perfect plan that can be played out and divinely orchestrated with His guidance and oversight in your life. Like a skilled master conductor who leads his musicians in a great symphony with all the different kinds of unique instruments, you have a very important part to play in the grand symphony of life. It is time for you to become aware of who you are and find out what part you were created to play.

Maybe secretly you have strong feelings that you know that you have been created for a specific and unique assignment in life, but you have been too afraid to come out into the open with it because you felt as if people would not see it the way you do. Or maybe you are just too afraid of the ridicule or persecution that you could potentially receive from others because of their views and mindsets about who they think you are and what they think you can or can't accomplish. Maybe you're concerned with the extent of how much of your own natural talents, abilities, and resources could carry you if you were to attempt to do what's in your heart. This is why it is so important for you to define who you are in God's grand design so that you can live out your life goals, dreams, visions and embrace a sense of purpose and destiny not with how you or others view yourself but how God views you.

If you have been feeling void and barren of the true meaning of life, and if your life has had the absence of significance, there is good news. Way down, deep on the inside of you, in the spiritual womb of your life, you have the ability and capacity to become impregnated with purpose and destiny by The Divine Seed of Heaven, God's perfect and holy beloved son Jesus Christ.

The word "seed" to which I am referring is taken from the Greek word "spérma," which simply means seed or seeds. It is the act of sowing seeds for an intended outcome of a particular harvest. It also refers to the seed cells derived from the male reproduction organ. It is the equivalent to the word "sperm." A male "gamete" reproductive cell called a "spermatozoon." The word "gamete" is the most significant word to the meaning of this book, and to your life, as it relates to your purpose and destiny. It simply means a mature sexual reproductive cell, such as a sperm or egg, which unites with another cell to form a new organism of new life.

Now I know it's a lot easier for women to relate to these kinds of ideas than it is for men. Although this may sound somewhat strange to men at first, please don't become uncomfortable and tune me out or dismiss these words right away. Please allow me some time to develop this concept as it is absolutely essential in helping you to understand one of the most powerful revelations I have ever discovered regarding ones purpose and destiny. Just as a man sows seed into the field and reaps a harvest of the seeds he has sown (providing he has sown into fertile ground); and just as a man sows his gamete (sperm cells) with an act of love and passion into the womb of a woman and creates a new life (providing that his seed has been sown into a healthy fertile womb); we too can become impregnated in the spiritual womb of our lives leading to a bountiful and fruitful harvest! That heavenly seed is called the Divine Seed of Heaven – Jesus Christ. He can impregnate you with heavens divine dream seeds. The seed He sows into the spiritual womb of your life releases God's desires and seeds of purpose, and destiny for your life. Not just for your life, but for the whole of humanity.

You Were Born for a Reason

Your birth parents (that is your blood father & mother) conceived you for a very specific reason. You are not an accident! No matter what events led up to and surrounded the day of your birth you were designed by God and born into this earth for a very specific and divine reason. Your birth mother carried you in her womb, then went into labor and painstakingly pushed to give birth to you for a special and unique reason. Your birthday was not a mistake! Your birth mother and your birth father may not have planned you, but your Heavenly Father not only planned for you, but He intentionally designed you and created you, and believe it or not, chose you even before you were born! You are one-of-a-kind, exceptional in every way, a designer's original. You have been fearfully and wonderfully made, right down to the number of hairs on your head (or lack thereof!). In the prophetic book of Jeremiah, God gives us some very powerful and revealing clues about our purpose and destiny: "Then the word of the LORD came to me (Jeremiah), saying: "Before I formed you in the womb I knew you; before you were born I sanctified you." (Jeremiah 1:4-5)

What God was saying here is that before you were even shaped in the womb He knew all about you. Even before you saw the very light of day, He had a holy and divine plan and purpose for your life. No matter what others have said about you, or what you might have even thought or said about yourself, you are a special person, just like snowflakes that fall from the heavens to the earth during winter, each are purely original, unique, and not the same. Just as no two human fingerprints are alike, you have something to do in this life that no one else can do, the way that only you can do it. You have something to say that no one else can say, the way that only you can say it. Never doubt that you were sent to earth with a definite and significant purpose. From your birth, you have been a VIP (a very important person) in the eyes of your Creator. I heard a wonderful Apostolic preacher friend of mine, Ed Delph,

President of NationStrategy say it like this: "There is a God. He is the true Master of the universe! That God has a Master plan and purpose. That Master plan is always working! And that Master plan includes you and the Master!"

With that mysterious truth in mind I believe that as you continue to passionately peruse the Master, concerning your purpose and destiny and as you continue searching the Holy scriptures and you keep reading on in this God inspired book that you will come to better understand more clearly God's divine master plan and purpose for your life. I truly believe that ALL things are divinely orchestrated in our life and that nothing, no matter how good, no matter how bad, nor how ugly things have played out in our lives that nothing happens by chance. God doesn't waste anything in our lives. He uses every circumstance and turns it all around for good no matter what has happened to us in the journey of life. There can be true meaning and purpose in a person's life no matter how good, bad, or ugly life has been to you.

We are not just supposed to be wandering aimlessly about the planet as lifeless zombie like creatures all wrapped up and stuck in the muck and the mire of life. We are not just taking up space on planet earth and wandering around throughout life trying to make the best of it. As much as I like Kenny Rogers's famous song, The Gambler, we are certainly not suppose to be living our life to the words of that tune: "you gotta know when to hold 'em – know when to fold 'em – know when to walk away – and know when to run."

We are not flat stuck with whatever hand that fate has dealt us. The reason why you and I live, breathe, move, and have our being is because there is a God in heaven who loves us and who has predestined our lives to be something special. He fashioned you and formed you in your mother's womb and has predestined you to live a fruitful, abundant, meaningful and happy life.

Do you even know what to do with your life yet? Does your life have a sense of destiny to it? Do you feel as if your life has true meaning and purpose? Maybe you're just starting out in the so-called game of life and you have a dream of doing something great in your early years. Perhaps you're still not sure what to do with your life although you have had tried many things and you are now approaching your latter years. Maybe you have already achieved some great personal or professional success in life, but in spite that you are still not happy with your life. Maybe you're not sure if what you are currently pursuing or doing every day of your life day in and day out, stuck in 'the grind' as they say is actually connected to your life's true purpose and destiny.

One of the first truths we must come to know in our life is that it's not what we 'do' in life that defines a man or woman's worth but it's 'who's we are' that makes us feel the greatest on the inside. Each and every one of us was chosen by God for greatness! God wants to take our humdrum lives and do something great with it! We must grasp the truth that we are destined and designed by God for greatness because until we do, we can never fully apprehend our divine potential and purpose in the earth. Again and again you will hear me say throughout this book that your birth was not by accident! Your purpose and calling is defiantly unique in every way. You needed to be born exactly when you were. You needed to be right here in the right now, alive in the twenty-first century!

With that said, who do you give the most of your life to, your time, talent, energy, and possessions? In other words, who gets most of the you in you? This is a very good foundational question when it comes to fulfilling and discovering your life's true purpose and destiny. I want you to know emphatically early on that your purpose and destiny is not orchestrated, directed, nor defined by what you do or don't do, but by who's you are! I'm talking about what or who owns us and possesses us.

Maybe you have a dream of doing something great with your life but you are just not sure how to get there. Or maybe you're like countless thousands of others in this world who are just plain board with their lives and just not really sure what to do to make their life better and more exciting. If you are reading this book, I want to say right now that I believe at this very moment in time that the Spirit of God has divinely led you. You are not just acting on a curious impulse or some crazy premonition. I believe you are being supernaturally influenced and led by the Holy Spirit. The Great I AM – the God of heaven and earth wants you to uncover His very real and unique plan for your life. It pleases Him to see you trying to connect to your creative destiny. From the very beginning of your life, God Himself formed and handcrafted you and your destiny and intended them to fit together as your hand fits firmly into a glove.

Do you have a dream in your heart, a vision, mission, calling, promise, an innovative business idea, or an undeniable burning passion deep within your soul? When you talk about your passions, do other people lovingly or facetiously call you a dreamer? Maybe you don't need others to say that to you, that's what you jokingly say about yourself. Maybe you're still in high school or attending college. Maybe you are a homemaker or a business professional, a blue-collar worker, an educator, a doctor, a lawyer, a politician, a CEO of a major corporation. Whatever your status or vocation, does what you 'do' satisfy and give you meaning and purpose in life, a sense of destiny being lived out and fulfilled? You may even be feeling right now, at this very moment, like you are about to burst with creative energy! Almost like you are about to explode because purpose and destiny is so 'big' on the inside of you that you are miserable doing anything else because it taints every other good thing you are doing in your life. In other words, you are never quite satisfied or totally happy and at ease with your life until you are doing what it is that drives you and pushes your passion button. There is such power and emotion that swells up in your life that it is almost making you miserable because you are not quite sure what to do about it or how to expresses yourself properly. In fact, you feel like an over filled helium balloon and you wish someone would just come along with a sharp pin to pop you and relieve some of your pressure from your inner creative feelings and desires.

If some of the questions I've posed and the personal emotional things I have mentioned describes you in any way, then more than likely, it was God Himself that placed those feelings deep on the inside of you by His Spirit. It's called Purpose and Destiny! All these feelings and emotions are part of your unique, one-of-a-kind, exceptional reason for being. Take it from me, you will never be completely happy until you are living out and doing' your reason for being.

Chapter 5
The Delivery Date of Your Destiny

In conception between a man and a woman there is a divine calculated moment in time, a "delivery date" designed by our Creator God for every fertile woman to go into labor, and to push, to give birth to the beautiful baby that has been wondrously growing on the inside the womb. On her final push, as that baby takes its first breath a new life is made a reality in the earth. So to, God has designed a birthing time, a "delivery date" for your purpose and destiny to be birthed forth in your life and made a reality in the earth.

Like in pregnancy, many of you have been carrying a promise (divine purpose) from God inside the spiritual womb of your life for a very long time with no indication of a delivery date. I believe because you have been led by the Holy Spirit to read this book at this precise moment in time, in this season of your life, you have come to the final hour of your labor pains and things are about to suddenly change.

Get ready, because your proverbial water just broke in the spiritual womb of your life, and just as the process goes with a woman ready to give birth, there is a shift, a change of seasons and a wonderful, powerful transformation coming to your life quickly! For those of you who are not spiritually pregnant yet, and want to be, and for those of you who have been feeling barren of any purpose and destiny in your life and feel unfertile and you desire to become pregnant with a heavenly pursuit of your true purpose destiny, the Holy Spirit can overshadow you. The Holy Spirit can cause the divine seed of truth to be placed on the inside of you as He did with Mary, the precious Mother of Jesus, and cause you to give birth to your heavenly purpose.

If you are feeling barren, old, and used up in your life, then you need to get ready as well because God can break the power of barrenness over your life today! Just like the song that declares this truth in the prophetic word given by the prophet Isaiah:

> "Sing, O barren, you who have not borne! Break forth into singing, and cry aloud, you who have not labored with child! For MORE are the children of the desolate than the children of the married woman," says the LORD. (Isaiah 54:1)

If you are feeling infertile to your purpose and destiny, God can literally break the curse of barrenness over your life both spiritually and physically. You will see your dreams fulfilled in this life even as God did a miracle with the many great women of old who suffered with barrenness in the Bible such as Sarah, Rebecca, Manoah's wife, Hannah, and Elizabeth just to name a few. I believe you have been led by the power of the Holy Spirit to read this book at this precise moment in time of your life. Why? Because God desires to expand your thoughts. He wants you to start thinking bigger, way bigger, than you have ever thought before. Get ready because I believe that as you read the next several pages of this destiny book you are going to become pregnant with the divine Seed of heaven. You're going to give birth to something so great, only the Holy Spirit will be able to help coach you through your time of spiritual labor and delivery just as He did with Mary the Mother of our Messiah Jesus.

> "And the angel answered and said to her, "The Holy Spirit will come upon you, and the power of the Highest will overshadow you; therefore, also, that Holy One who is to be born will be called the Son of God. Now indeed, Elizabeth your relative has also conceived a son in her old age; and this is now the sixth month for her who was called barren."
>
> Luke 1:35, 36

You see, the same Seed that was placed on the inside of Mary's physical womb, Jesus Christ is the very same Seed that the Holy Spirit places on the inside of your spirit when you become born again! Mary was overshadowed by the power of the Highest and became pregnant. Her purpose and destiny was part of God's Master plan: to help bear and bring forth the Son of God, the Savior of the entire world from her womb. Imagine that! Wow what an amazing and awesome life purpose!

As I have stated before, as we become pregnant within the spiritual womb of our lives with the divine Seed of heaven, Jesus Christ, we become pregnant spiritually with our very own purpose and destiny. A purpose that fits within God's master plan which then continues to help bear and manifest Jesus Christ, the Son of the living God, in the earth from one generation to the next. In a real sense, each of us is carrying salvation within us for our friends, family, and neighbors for an entire generation. Now that's BIG!

I would also like you to note in the book of Luke that God never leaves anyone out. Everyone is included when it comes to purpose and destiny. As He was infilling the young Mary and causing her to conceive and give birth to purpose and destiny, He was also infilling the old Elizabeth with purpose and destiny as well.

Of course, Elizabeth's destiny was to bear and give birth to the last and greatest of the Old Testament prophets, John the Baptist (see Matthew 11:10-11). John was the prophetic forerunner whose life purpose and destiny was to prophesy of and prepare the way for the New Testament fulfillment of the coming of the Messiah of Israel, the Savior of the world. Wow! What an amazing ministry opportunity that must have been.

> "And the Word became flesh and dwelt among us, and we beheld His glory, the glory as of the only begotten of the Father, full of grace and truth. John bore witness of Him and cried out, saying, "This was He of whom I said, 'He who comes after me is preferred before me, for He was before me.' And of His fullness we have all received, and grace for grace. For the law was given through Moses, but grace and truth came through Jesus Christ." (John 1:14-16)

> "And they asked him, saying, 'Why then do you baptize if you are not the Christ, nor Elijah, nor the Prophet?' John answered them, saying, 'I baptize with water, but there stands One among you whom you do not know. It is He who, coming after me, is preferred before me, whose sandal strap I am not worthy to loose...' The next day John saw Jesus coming toward him, and said, 'Behold! The Lamb of God who takes away the sin of the world! This is He of whom I said, 'After me comes a Man who is preferred before me, for He was before me.'" (John 1:25-26 & 29-30)

God had much more in store for Mary and her cousin Elizabeth than they ever dreamed or realized, God has so much more in store for your life than you ever dreamed or realized. You haven't been able to tap into it just yet, but as you continue to seek God and pursue your true purpose and destiny. Let the Word of God and this book become like a midwife in your life. A midwife comes alongside of a woman who is trying to give birth naturally. Let this book come alongside you and help you give birth to your destiny naturally. Let it help you breathe through all your contractions and the pain of your life and help to see you through to birthing and fulfilling your life's true purpose and destiny in Christ.

When is Birthing Time?

Just as a woman who has unselfishly given herself to her pregnancy and has taken great care both inwardly and outwardly for eight long months and is now in her ninth month, and cannot even remotely consider being pregnant or carrying her child a moment longer, you too find yourself asking, "When God? When? When is it birthing time? When will it come? I can't stretch much more! When will I know what my true purpose and destiny is?"

Even as these pleading words begin to roll off your lips, as you begin to work through the principles found in this book and from the Word of God you will suddenly begin to feel something strange beginning to happen to you, a sensation that you never felt before. 'It's the breaking forth of water! Your water just broke!' In a moment, you fully realize and are aware and declare from the depths of your being, "It's birthing time!" When you hear that powerful declaration of truth saying, "It's time," then the reality of those words immediately begin to take effect.

The contractions of labor start, and from your inner being you begin to hear the Holy Spirit say boldly, forcibly, and yet calmly; push, breathe... push, breathe. Then, after what seems like an eternity, but is really only a brief moment in the time span of your life, you are ready to give birth to something so big, so great, and powerful, that you feel as if you could never give birth to it on your own with your own strength. But somehow, someway you find the faith to believe that you can, and you muster up all the courage possible, the little bit of strength you have left, the power way down deep on the inside of you to continue pushing until... new Life is brought forth! Your purpose and destiny is finally born and has become a reality in your life and in the earth.

Life will never be the same for you again as things are about to suddenly change for you! Get ready! There is a shift and a change of seasons coming into your life. As you begin to open yourself up to this wonderful and powerful teaching you will become impregnated in the spiritual womb of your life and find that the Seed of heaven has penetrated the fertile egg of your divine destiny and you will begin to see your dreams come true. Just like the woman who has given birth to a newborn baby after many uncomfortable months of changing, stretching, and growing, and with all her labor pains, she finally gets to see the fruit of her toil. Her long awaited dream is made a reality as the bundle of new life is placed in her arms.

As I stated before, God wants to give you a deep seeded and deep rooted passion and a hunger to discover your purpose and destiny in Him. He not only wants you to discover it, but He also wants to give you the meaning of your life. My prayer is that this book will help you realize that you are not alone. Like a spiritual midwife, I pray that the principles contained in this book will help you gain the necessary instructions and information you need to be able to "push through" your time of spiritual labor so that you will be able to see your purpose and destiny from God come to pass before your very eyes.

Just as in the natural birthing process, when a woman gives birth to a precious life and wants to hold her miracle, I pray that your miracle from God will be something just as wonderful and magnificent for you to behold. When a woman with child finally gives birth to her dream in the delivery room after months and months of carrying that initial seed and gives that last and final push, she then sees (or beholds) the very thing that she has been laboring over for nine months. As the doctor or the midwife hands the baby to the woman, she then can not only gaze upon and hold in her bosom the full release of her promise, but also realize that it has surpassed every idea, thought, and dream she has ever had about what her baby would look like.

The reality of birth far surpasses anything she could have possibly imagined. One moment she was fully exhausted from the intense trial of her labor, and in the next she is completely energized and revitalized at the beautiful sight of her promise from God. Finally seeing her dream (that precious little life, her purpose and destiny) become a living reality. She instantaneously forgets all about her previous pain and toil, just one glance of her newborn baby, birthed new strength and new energy that she didn't have just moments earlier.

Listen, there is no such thing as the word ugly in a mothers eyes, to the new mother every child is beautiful in their own unique way. I pray that you will birth new passion, purpose, and energy to push through your time of intense spiritual labor pains so that when your dream (your purpose and destiny) is finally birthed and is manifested in your sight that it will surpass all your wildest dreams and imaginations.

Like many of you, I too wanted to know and discover my true purpose and destiny. I was one of those who got spiritually pregnant early in life, at the young age of 16. It all began directly after coming to know and falling in love with the Savior of the world and the lover of my soul Jesus Christ. Before then, I was miserable for quite some time in life until my purpose and destiny was uncovered through my salvation experience. Once my true purpose and destiny was revealed to me by the power of the Holy Spirit I have never been the same; I have never been more content and satisfied in my life. In fact, when my purpose and destiny was revealed to me I got the greatest sense that God was even more satisfied than I was! Since 1981 when I submitted my life to the Lordship of Jesus Christ I have been spiritually pregnant and in labor with the call of God upon my life. In fact, this book was conceived over 28 years ago as a direct result of being spiritually impregnated with the divine Seed of heaven, Jesus Christ. It has been an amazing and wonderful journey through the years seeing my purpose and destiny develop, unfold, and become birthed right before my very eyes.

The Lord gave me a strategic acrostic that spells out the word PUSH. Some people have coined this in Christendom with other meanings like; Pray Until Something Happens. I went with another positive application, however, and described it as Purpose Uncovered Satisfies Him. Of course the negative position of this acrostic would be: Purpose Undiscovered Saddens Him.

As I have stated before, we will discuss both of these weighty positions that God takes concerning our purpose and destiny in a spiritual and practical, hands-on way as it relates to how a woman conceives and goes through the many different stages of pregnancy. For the many ladies reading this book, you may find it very easy and natural to relate to the position and idea of giving birth, but for the men who may have picked this book up out of sheer curiosity you may be asking how in the world can giving birth relate and apply to me as a man?

The answer is that, in Christ, it still can and does relate every day. Ladies, it has been very difficult for me to write about all the facets of pregnancy since I am a man and have no idea what it's like to be pregnant for nine months, carrying a growing human being on the inside of my body, and having to give birth to that child. However, I do have tremendous respect and admiration for what you have to go through in order to be able to give birth to God's precious children of the earth.

I know what you're thinking right now ladies… you're thinking 'Yeah right! How on earth can this man even begin to relate to what I have gone through in order to give birth? Well, not to diminish your hardships in any way, but I think that the closet that I have ever come as a man in experiencing the pain and agony of child bearing was when I had to pass three kidney stones the size of a large grain of sand through a tiny tube the size of a little hair follicle. OUCH! The pain I felt was so absolutely excruciating and indescribable. So I can only imagine what it must be like for you to have to pass human being through such a small narrow birthing canal. I want every woman who has ever had the experience of childbearing, and those who will still yet have this experience in your life to realize just how vitally important you are in the grand scheme of life and creation.

God made you and chose you for a very unique purpose and destiny as well. God chose you to bring forth and birth forth destiny through your womb, His life and fruit in the earth. What an honor and a privilege this must be for you. The Bible describes this truth in the book of Romans Chapter 8:19 & 22: "For the earnest expectation of the creation eagerly waits for the revealing of the sons of God...For we know that the whole creation groans and labors with birth pangs together until now."

All of creation is waiting for you to become pregnant, even in the natural ladies. The created world itself can hardly wait for the children that are coming forth from your womb. I believe this verse is saying that everything in creation is being more or less held back; that God Himself reins it in until both creation and all the creatures (that's your children, my children, your life and mine, all of our destinies together) are ready to be birthed into the world. Held back so that they can be released for glorious times ahead, not just for our own personal lives, times, and seasons, but for all of creation's life, times and seasons.

What I am trying to say here is that your purpose and destiny is linked to the purpose and destiny of all of creation. Your actual birthday had great meaning and significance not just to us, to our families, and those who love us, but even more to God and to all of His Creation. This means that we all have a purpose and destiny to fulfill in God's grand design. He holds our purpose and destiny back and keeps it reined in until we are ready to seek Him for it. When we become impregnated, either in the natural or the spiritual realm, with His purposes and destiny for our lives, we are ready to give birth to that incredible destiny and release it into the earth. The whole earth is waiting for it (you) to be released! Isn't that amazing?

When you and I were born, it's as if all of creation rejoiced and sang Happy Birthday to us! Remember God has a master plan and we all play an important part in that plan. In fact, so much so, that the whole earth is waiting for you and your purpose and destiny to be released so it too can fulfill its own divine purpose and destiny.

Chapter 6
The Joy and The Pain

All around us we observe a pregnant creation. The difficult times of pain throughout the world are just simply birth pangs. Those pains are not only around us; they are within us as I'm sure those of you who have ever given birth within the last 50 years or so still have some flashbacks of that feeling. Motherhood brings great joy to many women, yet it is probably one of the greatest challenges they will ever have to face. Bringing a new life into the world is wonderful, but also terrifying and painful all at the same time. No mother can ever forget the marvel of holding a new life in her arms, or the remarkable experience of giving birth. Throughout history the most important contribution a woman had to offer society was the 'fruit of her womb.' No matter what anyone thinks they've been through, according to my studies of ancient childbearing giving birth to-day is nothing compared to past centuries when women had to endure all sorts of concoctions, contraptions and indignities on top of all the pain and trauma of childbirth. Of course, the pain in childbirth both past and present was a direct result and consequence of both Adam and Eve's dis-obedience to God's specific commands and instructions in the Garden of

Eden. In the next few verses, we read that the 'honeymoon in Paradise' comes to a screeching halt.

> Then the man said, "The woman whom You gave to be with me, she gave me of the tree, and I ate." And the LORD God said to the woman, "What is this you have done?" The woman said, "The serpent deceived me, and I ate." (Genesis 3:12-13)
>
> To the woman He said, "I will greatly multiply your sorrow and your conception; In pain you shall bring forth children; Your desire shall be for your husband, and he shall rule over you." Then to Adam He said, "Because you have heeded the voice of your wife, and have eaten from the tree of which I commanded you, saying, 'You shall not eat of it.' Cursed is the ground for your sake; in toil you shall eat of it All the days of your life. Both thorns and thistles it shall bring forth for you, and you shall eat the herb of the field. In the sweat of your face you shall eat bread till you return to the ground, for out of it you were taken; for dust you are, and to dust you shall return." (Genesis 3:16-19)

Long story short, God placed Adam and Eve in the Garden of Eden, the serpent enticed Eve to eat fruit from the tree of the knowledge of good and evil by telling Eve that she would become like God, knowing good and evil. After eating, she gave some of the fruit to her husband Adam who also ate it. Because of her disobedience, God said that He would "greatly multiply" a woman's experience in conception and that her pain in childbearing would "greatly increase."

Many changes have taken place through the centuries, and women now have more control than ever before over this fundamental part of their lives. Most Western women today have the power to choose when to start a family and to determine how large that family will be; pregnancy is often delayed until financial security is achieved. A woman can choose either to have her baby at home or in a hospital, and, with the increased number of elective caesareans in recent years, she may even decide when to have her baby so as to fit child birth conveniently into her busy schedule. She may choose to give birth standing, squatting, lying down, or even lying down under water in a pool or bath tub. Although this was certainly not the case for women in ancient biblical days, or even fifty years ago, women today are able to enter motherhood with a greater confidence knowing that both they and their infants are likely to survive the trauma of birth pains and reap the benefits of excellent healthcare thereafter.

As the due date approaches though, many women still feel apprehensive about their expected delivery date due to the concern of the pain they will ultimately feel at some point during the process of labor and delivery. That is why birth plans are discussed with great care with doctors, nurses, and midwives as various pain relieving methods are considered. The overall attitude towards birth has changed dramatically over the past fifty years or so, however, due largely to the sophistication of modern medicine. Women today expect not only to live through and face the pain of the birthing process with courage, but they also expect to enjoy the experience. Expert technology in surgical techniques, pain-killing drugs and hygienic surroundings are heavily relied upon and at times are even taken for granted.

No matter the modern technological advances, be they pain blockers, sophisticated birthing techniques, fancy private labor and delivery rooms and comfortable birthing bed's, we live on planet Earth which still operates under the law of sin and death. No one can ever ultimately 'take away' the inevitable pain of childbearing resulting from the judgment pronounced by God to woman in the Garden of Eden. The intense pain of childbearing is a vital part of the incredible process and experience called birth. Whether it's the pain of childbearing, or the pain that we all have experienced in this world at some point or another, the Spirit of God is still encouraging us and arousing us to continue to PUSH through the pain of labor in life so we can give birth to our purpose and destiny within.

It's like refreshing raindrops falling down from heaven. We fall from heavens vastness and land within our mothers wombs. Like divine seeds from heaven, sown by the Master Gardener into the fertile womb fields of our mothers. These seeds will not perish nor return to the master gardener empty handed or void, but will spring up into a harvest of life. The same holds true with the field of your life.

Remember, your life is not a mistake and is not void of purpose. No matter what the circumstances were that crowded into your life, you are a significant part of the master plan that God is creating in the world. Yes, sometimes the backdrop of that plan is dark and dreary, clouded with the pain and hurt of your personal experiences, riddled at times with great sorrow and grief, but these painful places can become the most powerful gift you can give to those living in their own dark shadows. Maybe your purpose and destiny is being birthed in the long dark night, but will someday become a powerful light that shines brightly into other people's darkness. That is why waiting does not diminish us in our purpose quest any more than waiting diminishes a pregnant mother. Why? Because just like a pregnant woman, we are enlarged and stretched in the waiting process. We, of course, don't see with our natural eye what is enlarging us, but the longer we wait, the larger we become, and the more joyful our expectancy is.

Are you becoming tired in the waiting? Then I have good news for you. The moment we get tired in the waiting for our purpose and destiny to be revealed, God's Spirit is right alongside us helping us. Maybe we don't know how or what to pray for in this time of waiting other than 'please...deliver me oh God!' The Bible says that He does our praying in and for us while we are pregnant with our purpose and destiny, making prayer out of our wordless sighs, and our aching painful groans.

He knows us far better than we know ourselves; He knows our pregnant condition, and keeps us present before God. That's why we can be confidently sure that every detail in our lives in God can and will ultimately be worked out for our good or turn into something good as it relates to our purpose and destiny.

> "Now He who searches the hearts knows what the mind of the Spirit is, because He makes intercession for the saints according to the will of God. And we know that all things work together for good to those who love God, to those who are the called according to His purpose."
>
> Romans 8:27, 28

Since the beginning of time, there have been so many great men and women of God who have gone before us that have experienced this same great and painful spiritual pregnancy. The Bible calls them "a great cloud of witnesses." Therefore we also, since we are surrounded by so great a cloud of witnesses, let us lay aside every weight, and the sin which so easily ensnares us, and let us run with endurance the race that is set before us...." (Hebrews 12:1)

Even as there have been many who have gone before us in their own spiritual pregnancy and birth pains there will continue to be countless numbers more of women and men who will yet continue to experience the very same thing after we are gone. In this important passage in Hebrews, the Apostle Paul strongly advises everyone to run their own race that is set before them with endurance like those who have done so before us. Like all those great historical men and women of the Bible who passionately perused and discovered their divine purpose and destiny in the earth, not to mention all those pioneers who blazed the way for us, this passage doesn't just speak of the influential lives and testimonies of the great cloud of witnesses recorded in biblical history. Rather, it speaks of all of those great men and women throughout the history of mankind who have passionately sought out and lived their divine purpose and destiny in their day.

Throughout history, the earth has been filled with men and woman who literally sacrificed all they had for their life's calling, and their true purpose and destiny. Many had their own blood shed painfully and gave their very lives for their heavenly purpose that God had called them to fulfill in the earth in their lifetime. As we look back over so many wonderful historical examples both in the past and in our present day, it should stir us up to get on with it! We need to get busy doing what it is that we have been called to do. We need to strip down from all our excuses and start running our race of purpose and destiny, and never quit! I would like to think that all those seasoned veterans that have gone before us are right now cheering us on from heaven as we are trying to connect to, give birth to, and fulfill our true purpose and destiny in our day.

Out of all the examples of those who have gone before us, there is none greater than that of the King of Kings Himself – Jesus Christ. We just need to keep our eyes fixed on Jesus, who both began and finished this race we're in. I want to encourage you to go to the Book – the Holy Bible – and study how He did it in the New Testament Gospels of Mathew, Mark, Luke, and John. Jesus never lost sight of where He was headed; He just saw that exhilarating finish line. In God and with God He could put up with anything along the way including the cross, the stripes upon His back, a crown of thorns upon His head, the nails in His hands and feet, the shame, and whatever was set before Him. Now He's there, seated in that place of honor, right alongside of God himself.

> ."..let us run with endurance the race that is set before us, looking unto Jesus, the author and finisher of our faith, who for the joy that was set before Him endured the cross, despising the shame, and has sat down at the right hand of the

> throne of God." (Hebrews 12:1, 2)

When you find yourself lagging in the pursuit of your purpose and destiny, go over His story again and again, that long litany of hostility and pain that He had to PUSH through. That alone will shoot some divine adrenaline into your soul. And ladies, guess what, there were no cutting edge epidural blocks for someone to administer to Jesus as the pain got to be too intense for Him. But He persevered and continued to PUSH through the labor pains of His true purpose and destiny so that He could give birth to our Salvation and give us all New Life.

Have you heard of the energy drink called NO FEAR? (that's one of my favorite pick-me-ups). You should hear me preach when I am all hopped-up on one of those before a Sunday service at my church, but it pales in comparison to the energy that can rush through your soul and body as you go over the greatest story ever told of NO FEAR in the Word of God! We need to constantly be reminded that in this all-out match against sin and depravity of this world, that there are others who have more than likely suffered far worse than you, to say nothing of what Jesus went through, all that horrible bloodshed! Don't let the excuse of feeling sorry for yourself hold you back anymore. Come out from the place of obscurity and shake it off! Do something great with your life while you still have time. Don't forget the greatest example of all time, Jesus Christ, the Righteous, our Savior and precious Redeemer who paid the ultimate price for His purpose and destiny, which was to redeem all mankind from their sins past, present, and future.

> "For consider Him who endured such hostility from sinners against Himself, lest you become weary and discouraged in your souls." (Hebrews 12:3)

From the very early development stages of this book my goal was to help you overcome your pain, weariness, and discouragement so that you too can come to know and clearly understand the enormous purpose and destiny that is growing and developing within you. I believe that you will soon discover the joy of your true purpose and destiny and it will help you to foresee past your pain (natural or spiritual) and help you to passionately pursue your tomorrow, your wonderful future!

His Pain Gave Birth to New Life

Although in the natural realm I may fall short in the birthing experience as a man, in the spiritual realm, I have had to carry in the womb of my life the spiritual fetus of divine purpose and destiny. As many women find themselves in labor for many hours in a hospital room pushing to give birth to a beautiful child, I too have experienced many years of long and intense spiritual labor pains in the womb of my life to give birth to my own beautiful God given purpose and destiny. Every moment of my natural life that I have spent PUSHING to give birth to my own life's purpose and destiny has been worth it.

I know that your spiritual birth pains will be worth it also. When Nicodemus (a wise religious man of his day, and a member of the Jewish Sanhedrin counsel) was asking Jesus about how a man could receive Salvation. The age-old purpose and destiny question arose in his life and Jesus himself used the very same female birthing analogy (that I am trying to use in this book) to help Nicodemus understand the gift of Salvation. Let's take a look: "There was a man of the Pharisees named Nicodemus, a ruler of the Jews. This man came to Jesus by night and said to Him, "Rabbi, we know that You are a teacher come from God; for no one can do these signs that You do unless God is with him." Jesus answered and said to him, "Most assuredly, I say to you, unless one is born again, he cannot see the kingdom of God." Nicodemus said to Him, "How can a man be born when he is old? Can he enter a second time into his mother's womb and be born?" Jesus answered, "Most assuredly, I say to you, unless one is born of water and the Spirit, he cannot enter the kingdom of God. "That which is born of the flesh is flesh, and that which is born of the Spirit is spirit. "Do not marvel that I said to you, 'You must be born again." (John 3:1-7)

Jesus was trying to explain to Nicodemus that Purpose and destiny is not just grasped by the mind but like the womb of a fertile woman a man's sperm finds it home inside a woman's womb and she becomes impregnated and procreates.

The same is true when Jesus finds His way inside a believer's heart; we become impregnated with the divine Seed of heaven (Jesus Christ) and we are birthed into the kingdom of God, we become 'Born Again' as the scriptures say. Jesus is waiting for all of us to receive Him (the divine Seed of heaven) into our hearts (the spiritual wombs of our lives) so that we can become impregnated by His Holy Spirit. As we do, we can grow, mature, and stretch with His divine plan and purposes for our lives and He can help us give birth to our new life in God through His Son, Jesus Christ whereby we can receive that new life by becoming born again of the Spirit of God. Through that spiritual birthing process if you will, we can PUSH through the yoke of sin and death and enter into the Kingdom of God and discover God's wonderful master plan for our lives. The Bible tells us that all faith is released by the power of the Holy Spirit as we hear God's Word. The Lord imparts His creative ability and strength into the hearts of those who earnestly desire Him and they become impregnated with the plans and purpose of God. The example of this is found in Romans 10:17, "So then faith comes by hearing, and hearing by the word of God..."

But not everybody is ready for this, ready to see and hear and act upon this wonderful truth. Maybe there are those of you who are reading this book who are wondering the very same thing, "am I ready yet?" I believe you ARE ready! I believe you were ready the very second you picked up this book in sheer curiosity to see what truth (if any) was contained on the inside to help you discover and fulfill your own purpose and destiny.

I believe that it was worth taking every bit of the time from your busy life to read these pages and to continue reading on. If you even got this far along in the book, then I believe deep down in your spirit you know this to be true. In the Word of God the prophet Isaiah was wondering if anyone was listening to his preaching: He said: "Does anyone care, God? Is anyone listening and believing a word of what I am telling them?"

The point is this, I am speaking the truth to you today and before you can even begin to discover your own life's purpose and destiny, you have to be able to trust, and before you can trust, you have to be able to listen. So the question is, are you listening to what the Spirit of God is trying to say to you through the teaching in this book? If I wasn't teaching Christ's Word, but some other form of religion, wisdom, or man's philosophies then there would be nothing to listen to, but I am speaking the truth of the Word of God in love to those who truly want to hear and discover their true purpose and destiny. If you are ready to trust, then listen and receive the God of destiny – Jesus Christ, God's One and only begotten Son is ready to help you as He helped Nicodemus so long ago. In fact, Jesus has helped countless numbers of men and women throughout the ages and He can do the very same for YOU right here and right now by just simply saying a little prayer with me. When you do, Jesus will come into your heart (the spiritual womb of your life) and save you, heal you, deliver you, fill you with His Holy Spirit and set you free, and impregnate you with truth in your heart and soul. He will fill you up with His presence, His power, and will divinely set your feet onto the path of your God ordained purpose and destiny.

Lord, I pray that you bless the one reading this, as well as their family with long and healthy lives. Jesus, make Yourself so real to the one who is praying with me right now and do a quick work in their heart. May they even feel Your very presence overshadow them as we pray together today. If they have not received Jesus Christ as their Lord and Savior, I pray they will do so right here and now!

If you are one of those who would like to receive the gift that God has for you today, and you would like for the Holy Spirit to fill you up with truth and set your feet upon the path of your life's divine purpose and destiny, then say this prayer after me with your whole heart – not just with your mind (not just your intellect). Say it with your lips out loud so you can hear yourself praying:

> Dear Lord Jesus, come into my heart. Forgive me of my sin. Wash me and cleanse me. Set me free. Jesus, thank You that You died for me. I believe that You are the Son of God. I believe that you have risen from the dead and that You're coming back again for me. Fill me with the Holy Spirit, give me a hunger and a passion for the things of God. Give me an unquenchable desire to know and to fulfill my true purpose and destiny in Jesus. Give me a real and genuine concern for the lost and a holy boldness to preach the gospel of Jesus Christ. I'm saved; I'm born again, I'm forgiven and I'm on my way to Heaven because I have Jesus in my heart. In the mighty name of Jesus I pray, Amen.

As a minister of the Gospel of Jesus Christ, I tell you today that all of your sins are forgiven. Always remember to run to God and not from God because He loves you and has a great purpose and destiny for your life! Now you are truly ready to discover and fulfill your divine purpose and destiny! The book of Psalms describes how wonderful and special each one of us truly is, and how purposeful we were made by the hands of a creative God:

"For You formed my inward parts; you covered me in my mother's womb. I will praise You, for I am fearfully and wonderfully made; marvelous are Your works, and that my soul knows very well. My frame was not hidden from You, when I was made in secret, and skillfully wrought in the lowest parts of the earth. Your eyes saw my substance, being yet unformed. And in Your book they all were written, the days fashioned for me, when as yet there were none of them...." (Psalms 139:13-16)

This passage is absolutely vital for us to truly embrace and to come to know and understand our purpose and destiny. God uses this beautiful Psalm to describe in great detail how He shaped us first inside, then out; and how He formed us in our mother's womb. If you have ever watched a time-lapsed documentary of how a fetus actually develops and grows on the inside of a woman's body, you see how absolutely breathtaking and marvelous it really is! What an amazing creator He is!

God planned and created the whole birthing process, not just in the human kingdom, but as well as with the animal, insect, and plant kingdoms. They all must begin with a seed, so there is no doubt that the Lord knows you and I inside and out. He knows every bone in our body; He knows exactly how we were made, bit by bit, piece by piece, how we were sculpted from nothing into something. Like an open book, He watched you and I grow in the cocoon of our mother's womb from conception to birth; all the stages of our life were spread out before Him, the days of our life were prepared before we had ever lived.

That is a mind blower isn't it? But it's all true! You see, when a person taps into and uncovers their purpose and destiny (their reason for being) it releases the greatest potential within them in the world. That potential becomes a blazing hot burning passionate fire on the inside of them and that passionate fire becomes the vehicle that transports them and catapults them into their final destination in life, their destiny, the very reason why they were born. All this starts with believing, having faith and believing in God, believing that He has a wonderful plan for you to fulfill in this life, and believing that He has created you with the potential it will take to complete the special and unique mission and call upon your life.

Chapter 7
Believing Releases Our Potential

One of the most fascinating and beautiful women on the planet is my lovely wife Phaedra. She is the most precious, faithful, gifted, talented, and strongest women I have ever met in my life. She has been the joy of my life, my best friend, and my strength in many seasons of weakness. Together we are raising three beautiful children. One daughter Abigail Rose who is 6 years old, and two boys, Michael David who is 10 years old and Brian James who is 21 years old and recently married to his lovely wife Bryanna. Brian is also currently serving as a Military Police officer in the United States Army. They are all beautiful children each one having their own miracle story. There is a glorious testimony for each one of my children's lives that relate to purpose and destiny in a very dynamic way.

Besides my wonderful parents Jim & Racheal Alton, my wife Phaedra has been one of the key people in my life who have not only supported my dreams but she truly believes in them and believes in me to fulfill them. In many ways, she has become my personal spiritual midwife through many years of my own ministerial stretching and leadership development.

I don't know what I would do without her influence in my life. I know that without her strength, patience, and prayers I would have never been able to give birth to a huge part of my own life's unique purpose and destiny.

I am a minister with an apostolic and prophetic heart and ministry (Apostolic in mantle and anointing not in church denomination). I am the founding Senior Pastor and Chancellor of a wonderful congregation and ministry training center called Desert Rose Community Church & Gateway International Bible Institute in beautiful Glendale, , Arizona. I have helped give birth to and fathered many 'spiritual children' throughout the course of my 29 years in ministry. Many of them are miracle children as well, and I wouldn't have enough time to write about all of their stories in the pages of this book. They too have believed in me, in my calling, vision, ministry, and they have helped me to personally come to know and better understand my own God given potential.

They, along with my parents, my wife and children, have believed in the potential on the inside of me. They all have played a part in helping me to grow and to give birth to my life's purpose and destiny; in fact, they are why I find true fulfillment in this life. The key was having someone (even if it was just one person) to believe in me. These precious ones stood believing with me and that has made all the difference in the world. Through being their pastor, loving them, and trying to serve them in Christ, I have constantly been reminded that we are the sum total of all the people we have known, met, loved, and learned from, especially from those who have taken the time and interest to acknowledge and encourage the potential locked up on the inside. Praise God for those who have believed in us, and hoped with us to see our dreams come true.

My advice to you is that if you have someone (anyone) in your life right now that is doing that for you (believing with you) then you really need to cherish them because many times they can be few and far between. All Children of God have been given great potential from God to be, to do, and to receive all He wants to give them. It is God's chief desire to bless us and to give us good gifts from above for our enjoyment; in fact I believe that it brings God just as much enjoyment as it does us. The book of James tells us: "Every good gift and every perfect gift is from above, and comes down from the Father of lights, with whom there is no variation or shadow of turning." (James 1:7) Having faith pleases God but believing with God releases our greatest potential.

> "By faith Enoch was taken away so that he did not see death, "and was not found, because God had taken him"; for before he was taken he had this testimony, that he pleased God. But without faith it is impossible to please Him, for he who comes to God must believe that He is, and that He is a rewarder of those who diligently seek Him." (Hebrews 11:5-6)

I believe the key to Enoch pleasing God so much and the result of his supernatural translation into heaven wasn't just that he had faith in God and walked with him, but that Enoch's faith believed with God. Believing with God brought great pleasure to the Lord which released the greatest potential in his life. In this case, that potential brought about a miracle translation that had never been done before in Enoch's generation or in the history of mankind before him. As I described before, it's like when you have someone in your life who believes in you as a person and they really see the potential that is in you to accomplish something wonderful in your life. They believe in your potential to accomplish something great and they continue to encourage you, they believe right along with you as you are believing, and that in itself releases the power of potential within you to begin to excel and succeed.

I think it is very much like how a husband comes along side his wife during her pregnancy. He can in no way begin to understand or identify what his wife is going through. He cannot totally understand all the changes going on in her body, but he continues to stand with her. He holds her hand through times of discomfort and difficulty, and is there helping to coach her along with encouraging words and taking each breath one-by-one right along with her saying "you can do this!" Men, you have the wonderful opportunity to stand by your wife and believe with her to help encourage her to release her greatest potential developing on the inside of her. You have to help her withstand the inevitable pain and endure the hours of labor to give birth to that wonderful miracle child!

What is potential? It means, 'existing in possibility, capable to develop, something that can develop or become a reality.' God has given every believer a great potential that exists within their spirit. This potential can develop on the inside of us to help us be able to become, to do, and to receive every good and perfect gift from above, essentially all that God offers us in His Word. Enoch not only had faith in God, but he believed with God and achieved the potential to be translated right into heaven to join the entire heavenly host in praising God 24/7. That is so cool! I want you to know today that Jesus knows your full potential, He doesn't look at what you are so much as He looks at what you can become with His help. The saddest words ever spoken or even written of others are "What might have been?" or "I wonder what could have been?" or "Only if." I call them the "should-a-would-a-could-of's." The Lord knows what you can achieve, don't underestimate Him.

When 16-year old Eliza married a 20-year old tailor, he had never been to school before. Others might have written his education off as a lost cause, but Eliza didn't. She believed in him and taught him to read, write, and to spell. Yes, those days were very difficult for her, but he proved to be a fast learner. In fact, he learned so well that years later he was elected President of the United States! When he ran for a second term he lost, but refused to give up. Instead, he won a seat in the U.S. Senate. Who was this old tailor that Eliza took the time to believe with?

It was our 17th President, Andrew Johnson. You see, Eliza saw what Andrew could become, just Like God sees what you and I can become. He sees our potential! On New Year's Day, 1929, Georgia Tech played the University of California in the Rose Bowl. In that game, a man named Roy Riegels recovered a fumble for California. Somehow, he became confused and started running 65 yards in the wrong direction. One of his teammates, Benny Lom, had to try and outrun him and was able to down him just before he scored for the opposing team. When California attempted to punt, Georgia Tech blocked the kick and scored a safety, which was the ultimate margin of victory.

That incredibly strange play came in the first half of the game, and everyone who was watching the game was asking the same question, "What will Coach Nibbs Price do with Roy Riegels in the second half?" The men filed off the field and went into their locker room. They sat down on the benches and on the floor, all but Riegels. He put his game towel around his shoulders, sat down in a corner, put his face in his hands, and cried like a baby.

If you have ever played football, you know that a coach usually has a great deal to say to his team during half time, some good words, and some not so good. That day Coach Price was quiet. No doubt he was trying to decide what to do with Riegels. Then the timekeeper came in and announced that there were three minutes left before they were suppose to go back out onto the field to play the second half of that game. Coach Price looked at the team and said simply, "Men, the same team that played the first half will start the second." The players got up and started out, all but Riegels, he did not budge. The coach looked back and called to him again; still he didn't move. Coach Price went over to where Riegels sat and said, "Roy, didn't you hear me? The same team that played the first half will start the second."

Then Roy looked up, his cheeks were wet with tears and said: "Coach, I can't do it to save my life. I've ruined you, I've ruined the University of California, and I've ruined myself. I couldn't face that crowd in the stadium to save my life!"

Then Coach Price reached out and put his hand on Roy's shoulder and said to him, "Roy, get up and go on back; the game is only half over." Roy Riegels went back, and those Georgia Tech men will tell you that they have never seen a man play football as amazing as Roy Riegels played that second half. Some of you need to get up and play like you never have before; God has a great future ahead of you. The game of life is not over yet. It's only half over for some and maybe just beginning for others but you need get on with it! It's time to give birth to your life's purpose and destiny.

Now the release of this potential that we are discussing here is the responsibility of the Holy Spirit. Better yet, we could say the release of the truth that births potential within us is the responsibility of the Holy Spirit, but the activation of this potential is the responsibility of the believer.

We as believers have to act on the truth that has already been revealed to us. We are not held responsible for the truth that we don't know, but we are held responsible for the truth that we do know. Therefore believing in the truth that has already been revealed to us is in fact, believing with God. It is the only method that we have to be able to release the God inspired kind of potential in our lives.

There are two kinds of potential: one is the "God potential" and the other is "self potential." When we operate in the God potential, we become all that God wants us to be and as a result, we enjoy His approval and satisfaction. Self potential seeks to make us go by what we think and feel. Sadly, so many of us are determined to be what we want to be, to do what we want to do, and get what we want to get no matter what! In our human effort, we seek after things that please the flesh and our carnal mind and we try to force things to happen and take place in our lives. Then when we have messed everything up and its crisis time in our life we demand that God 'do something' according to our desires. Self potential can bring worry, defeat, confusion, doubt, frustration, depression, discouragement, unbelief, and more. Self potential seeks to develop what the human nature wants, not what God wants. If all we are doing is living for self and essentially serving our self life then all we can do is struggle with the plans and purposes of God in our lives because things are not happening the way we are demanding for them to happen. This prevents the God potential from developing on the inside of us.

I think it was Bob Dylan who sang the song "We All Gotta Serve Somebody." We are either going to serve the Lord, the world, the flesh, or the devil but we're all "gonna have to serve somebody." It's God's desire that we seek to serve His kingdom and not any other.

> "But seek first the kingdom of God and His righteousness, and all these things shall be added to you. "Therefore do not worry about tomorrow, for tomorrow will worry about its own things. Sufficient for the day is its own trouble." (Matthew 6:33, 34)

Just as a fetus develops in its mother's womb, God's potential brings full development of our purpose and destiny. His potential comes from salvation; it brings deliverance and preservation, grace with blessings, the fruit of the Spirit, and the gifts of the Spirit. In these things, God's potential is released out of us as a baby is released from its mother's womb.

During pregnancy, a woman lives a life a self denial and sacrifice for her baby alone. So too, God's potential working on the inside of us brings self denial and sacrifice for God alone. This is the victory that overcomes self. God's potential develops us for Himself alone, and for our whole life as a believer. Believing with God gives us the highest ambitions in life. The most mistakes are made when we compromise with the highest goals that God has for us, most of the time it's when we settle for what is of lesser value.

This happens to us when we are more concerned with appeasing self and what others want for us. We should not settle with what appeals to us, but what appeals to God. God's choice for us does not come to us through human desire, but through spiritual desire. Having a passion for God's purposes in our lives can be the drive and the Godly ambition that causes us to fulfill His desire in our life and not our own. Godly ambition is the desire to achieve. Believing with God gives us a desire to only want what He has planned for us, but ambition is the ability to achieve the highest goal set for us by God.

This ability helps us to reach beyond the stress and strain of life and catapults us into God's dimension. In this dimension, all accomplishments are directed by God. All advancements are provided by God, and all credibility and success is determined by God alone. Believing with God develops our success in life. Success is defined as "outcome, result, attainment, accomplishment, achievement, and victory."

Now, all of these definitions describe success, but true success is when all these things come forth because God is imparting them to us through believing with Him. I believe this kind of success can only become truly active with us as we gain Godly approval, spiritual determination, and divine insight concerning His plan and purpose for our lives. Believing with God is a direct connection with God. We can all personally have direct contact with the Lord through Jesus Christ. No human being stands in for us with God. God desires direct attention from us, so He can perform in us, with us, and through us on a personal basis.

> "For there is one God and one Mediator between God and men, the Man Christ Jesus…." (I Timothy 2:5)

No success can be attained without our knowledge of God's approval.

What is approval? It is acceptance, blessing, endorsement, and favorable backing of His opinion, it is accepting His opinion as completely satisfactory. Every human being desires these traits that exist in approval. Approval brings forth a drive that causes one to accomplish what is desired for success, but like with every good thing that has been given to man to use for good, man can take it to an unhealthy extreme.

Some people can take a desire for approval and develop what is called an "approval addiction." Always building their lives on what other people like or dislike, approve of or disapprove of. Believing with God brings about a healthy need for approval which becomes stimulation and motivation to be something for God based on His approval only. Approval is recognition; recognition means "to acknowledge with a show of appreciation." This kind of recognition gives us a successful attitude. To be backed by God in our lives is divine recognition and the approval we need for our success. The only recognition and approval we need in life is God's.

Secondly, we must have spiritual determination. This is God's impartation to us through His Spirit. What is determination? It is acting to decide definitely, the power to decide, a fixing of a position, direction or tendency, completing a process with results, bringing to conclusion. The word impartation simply means 'sharing.' When we believe with God, He shares with us His determination. This allows Him to make decisions for us, and gives us direction through His Holy Spirit.

Thirdly, we need divine insight concerning His plan for our lives. What is insight? It is the capacity to discern the true nature of a situation; penetration; the act or outcome of grasping the inward or hidden nature of things, the ability to perceive in an intuitive manner. When we believe with God, He gives us insight regarding His plan for our lives. This reminds me of the intuitive nature that a woman has when she is pregnant. Often times via a woman's intuitive nature she is able to discern way before the determination of an ultrasound test what the sex of her baby is. Women have been given by God a special kind of a divine insight or knowing of the inward hidden things.

When we believe with God, we are successful in Him. How do we know we are successful in Him? By allowing Him to begin to use us in our purpose and destiny it makes us successful in Him. What will help us to believe we are successful in Him? We must become dependable, reliable, faithful, consistent, and pliable. All of these things make up the ingredients of success. Let's look at each word we just discussed and see what is implied:

- **Dependable:** capable of being depended upon, placing trust or reliance upon, tried and true, trustworthy, secure, responsible, and confident.
- **Reliable:** having qualities that merit confidence, unerring and proven, confirmed, giving the same result on successive trials.
- **Faithful:** steadfast in affection or allegiance, firm in adherence to promises, or in observance in duty, true to the facts, unquestionable.
- **Consistent:** possessing firmness, harmonious regularity or steady continuity, showing steady conformity to character, free from irregularity, variation, or contradiction.
- **Pliable:** supple enough to bend freely or repeatedly without breaking, yielding readily to others, adjustable to varying conditions, being easily influenced, adaptable.

These words reveal the depth or success that is performed in and through us. Success is found in the attainment of these words being activated in our everyday lives. Jesus in us makes us capable of all these qualities. Believing with God allows what these words mean to be fulfilled in us. All of these words are very expressive in revealing what Jesus is causing us to be, as we peruse our purpose and destiny in Him, He confirms us as true. He makes us firm in adherence to promises. He gives us the desire and drive to show a steady conformity to His character. He develops us to be responsible, and He performs in us to help us to be adjustable without breaking. When we see these qualities in action in our lives then, we know that believing with God is making us successful in God and we are moving closer and closer to our purpose and destiny. Believing only wants God's very best. You see, when we believe we receive God's very best. When we refuse to believe, we reject the best God has for us and we accept what we want or what other people want for us as a substitute. Believing only accepts what God wants and God always wants the very best in all things.

> "Now may the God of peace who brought up our Lord Jesus from the dead, that great Shepherd of the sheep, through the blood of the everlasting covenant, make you complete in every good work to do His will, working in you what is well pleasing in His sight, through Jesus Christ, to whom be glory forever and ever. Amen."
>
> Hebrews 13:20, 21

What does 'very best' mean? 'The choicest, the cream of the crop, the best prize, and top notch'! It is what God chooses, not what we tell Him we want. It is that which will honor and exalt the Lord in our lives not ourselves or our own ingenuity and strength. It means to give God all the glory in our lives, and exalt His nature in us when we are able to accomplish anything noteworthy. When we believe with God, we allow God to perform His top choice in us. When we do not believe, we go our way to make our own choices happen. Unfortunately, I have proven this to be true too many times in my own life. How about you? Many times our own choice is not God's best choice for our lives. We try to force things to happen, and this will get you nowhere very fast! You see, believing does not place any force on God to make something happen. Believing grants God time and privilege to bring things together in our lives. Believing sets God in motion to bring the special pick of things for us, the choicest, the cream of the crop if you will. The biggest struggles come to our lives when we try seeking our own wants and desires and we try to make them happen in our own strength apart from God. When God's best is being developed in us, we become submissive to Him in all things. We do not demand what we want, but we become willing to allow Him to perform what He wants. So many people in the world desire God to give them what they want without waiting for Him to perform what He wants for them. Then, in their own strength apart from God, they press forward in getting what they want and then they quickly realize that it wasn't everything they had hoped it would be. They become disillusioned and depressed over all the time, talent, money, and energy they have spent on chasing after things that don't satisfy their soul the way they had hoped they would. Believing with God allows God to have what He wants in us. Sadly, many have the carnal determination to get what they want at any cost. When something doesn't happen one way, they take off in another direction to try and bring to pass what they want. This is why there is so much frustration taking place in people's lives.

> "Where do wars and fights come from among you? Do they not come from your desires for pleasure that war in your members? You lust and do not have. You murder and covet and cannot obtain. You fight and war. Yet you do not have because you do not ask. You ask and do not receive, because you ask amiss, that you may spend it on your pleasures." (James 4:1-3)

> "But you are a chosen generation, a royal priesthood, a holy nation, His own special people, that you may proclaim the praises of Him who called you out of darkness into His marvelous light; who once were not a people but are now the people of God, who had not obtained mercy but now have obtained mercy. Beloved, I beg you as sojourners and pilgrims, abstain from fleshly lusts which war against the soul...." (I Peter 2:9-12)

So many people are too busy listening to what others are saying and not taking the time to hear what God is speaking. God wants us to listen to Him on a personal basis. He does not need a human go-between for us. He can and will speak to us on His own, if we will only listen. Lastly, in believing with God peace has a chance to reign. The Greek word for peace means: 'exemption from the rage and havoc of war, the absence or end of strife, harmony, tranquility, security, prosperity, a state of health or well-being, rest, a state of being untroubled or undisturbed, well-being.' When you need peace, look to some of these scriptures:

> "Peace I leave with you, My peace I give to you; not as the world gives do I give to you. Let not your heart be troubled, neither let it be afraid." (John 14:27)
>
> "Therefore, having been justified by faith, we have peace with God through our Lord Jesus Christ." (Romans 5:1)
>
> "But the fruit of the Spirit is love, joy, peace, longsuffering, kindness, goodness, faithfulness." (Galatians 5:22)
>
> ."..and the peace of God, which surpasses all understanding, will guard your hearts and minds through Christ Jesus." (Philippians 4:7)
>
> "And let the peace of God rule in your hearts, to which also you were called in one body; and be thankful." (Colossians 3:15)
>
> "For He himself is our PEACE...." (Ephesians 2:14)

Peace gives us the assurance that war and strife are gone. Before we were born again in Jesus Christ the war we were fighting was with God. Now, in Christ Jesus our Savior we exist upon a position of peace. This means that we are not at war any longer. We are standing in victory! When we believe with God we are standing firm.

Chapter 8
Trauma Can Abort Your Destiny

About 3 years ago I began to see people around me experience a downsizing (including my own ministry) having to move into smaller, more cramped uncomfortable places. The Lord said to me, "This appears to be a step backwards, but when a baby is being born, it is moved from a large place (the womb) into a small place (the birth canal). It has to transition from a large place to a smaller place before it can come into the larger place that is ordained for it. If there is a struggle against the process by the mother or the baby, both the mother and the baby will experience more discomfort and trauma. In childbirth when it is 'time' the baby will come even when the mother or the baby are not ready mentally, physically or spiritually.

Before experiencing full time ministry I spent many years in the Behavioral Health field. At one time in my career I was a lead supervisor over three outpatient clinics working alongside Psychiatrists, nurses, and directing therapists, and case management staff. We all worked together as a team for the appropriate care and treatment goals for the clients we served.

During that time I remember having to attend some mandatory continued education classes offered by the Psychiatric management company I worked for. In their material, there was a concept they covered called "External Trauma." They teach that external trauma can happen to a person before birth. It comes from the feelings of not being wanted.

All the fighting, screaming, negative words, etc, that happen outside the womb during the development stages of life medical studies have discovered that babies will fight against the process of birth. This can result in a long unnecessary labor and pain for women because the baby has fear instilled into it. Worse yet the baby can have major medical issues, and become stillborn. If you have just been told by your doctor that you are pregnant how have you and your husband readied yourself and your baby for the process?

What about your spiritual pregnancy? Has God's baby (your purpose and destiny) been hearing words of fear or words of faith? Have you been embracing and nurturing it with love, anticipation, and the solid food of the Word? Or has it had to gain its sustenance from junk food or the sweet delicacies that tickle your ears and place you in denial of spiritual realities. This is perhaps worse than exposing your baby to fear, emotional or physical abuse. There is a position that is conducive to an easier birth.

Now for those who have had babies, they will tell you that there is nothing easy about the process. Then talk with those who have gone into labor with a baby in the wrong position. Here is where the word "Reposition" comes into play. In a natural pregnancy, the womb is roomy enough to allow a fetus to change position, rotate, and come out head first. If the baby is not in this position it is breech. For the sake of the mother and the child, the doctor must turn or re-position the baby.

We should be crying out for the Lord to enlarge our capacity to hold those things that He would want to bring forth in and through us. In this season, we cannot afford to allow unbelief to malnourish and abort our baby (your purpose and destiny). We are the sons of God that He wants to birth forth on the scene. We are carrying dreams and visions that God has entrusted us to carry in our womb. Once we learn and work with the process, it becomes easier to give birth to what He has placed inside of us.

There is a great parallel between the natural and spiritual birthing process. The first few children a woman has, may seem tough, but before long, she will become a pro at birthing. The same holds true spiritually the first few things we give birth to as it relates to our purpose and destiny may seem long, painful, and difficult for us, but before long, we will become better equipped at birthing God's plan for our health, for our marriages, families, businesses, and ministries, whatever lies ahead for us. Since your spiritual destiny will be great, you must enlarge the capacity of your tent, and then be ready to extend your boundaries.

> "For your Maker is your husband, The LORD of hosts is His name; and your Redeemer is the Holy One of Israel; He is called the God of the whole earth. For the LORD has called you like a woman forsaken and grieved in spirit, like a youthful wife when you were refused," Says your God. "For a mere moment I have forsaken you, but with great mercies I will gather you. With a little wrath I hid My face from you for a moment; but with everlasting kindness I will have mercy on you," Says the LORD, your Redeemer." (Isaiah 54:5-8)

Isaiah is a great book if you are feeling lost and confused, grieved and forsaken, broken and stretched to capacity. Very much like how a woman who has borne a child, she is stretched. The labor is neither as long nor as hard as it once was. Her body becomes acclimated and she begins to learn to flow with the order of things that come with birthing. She begins to overcome the sense of impatience and realizes that there is a time and season for the child to come forth. She begins to realize that the waiting is a time of preparation for her and the child that will come. Her tolerance and strength for carrying and birthing becomes limitless; the second and subsequent babies become easier. She looks forward to the reward of seeing the miracle of birth and seeing the child grow in the likeness of herself and her husband. At some point, the ability of birthing natural children ends because of the physical weariness and age of the women's body.

However, in the spiritual realm there is no end to giving birth because there is no limit of time and strength in this realm. The more children that are birthed, the more built in babysitters there are. The babysitters are taught supernaturally by the mothers (mentors) to expand their abilities to bear children and thus begin a birthing process of their own. They will be taught to perfect the process to increase the ability to bear children. Our Maker is our Husband and a fertile Husband is He. For the Lord says, "I am looking for people who will make their profession and confession birthing My will, My dreams, My visions, and My next generation. Many become weary before the real multiplication begins. It begins with the second generation."

May it become for you like Isaiah 66:7-14:

> "Before she was in labor, she gave birth; Before her pain came, She delivered a male child. Who has heard such a thing? Who has seen such things? Shall the earth be made to give birth in one day? Or shall a nation be born at once? For as soon as Zion was in labor, she gave birth to her children. Shall I bring to the time of birth, and not cause delivery?" says the LORD. "Shall I who cause delivery shut up the womb?" says your God. "Rejoice with Jerusalem, And be glad with her, all you who love her; Rejoice for joy with her, all you who mourn for her; That you may feed and be satisfied With the consolation

of her bosom, That you may drink deeply and be delighted With the abundance of her glory." For thus says the LORD: "Behold, I will extend peace to her like a river, And the glory of the Gentiles like a flowing stream. Then you shall feed: On her sides shall you be carried, And be dandled on her knees. As one whom his mother comforts, So I will comfort you; And you shall be comforted in Jerusalem." When you see this, your heart shall rejoice, And your bones shall flourish like grass; The hand of the LORD shall be known to His servants, And His indignation to His enemies."

Get Me to the Delivery Room!

How many of you remember the day you found out that you or your spouse was pregnant? The numbness that settled over you and then excitement came in waves. You and your husband lay beside each other that night staring at the ceiling as your thoughts raced by. You began discussing all the changes that would imminently be coming to your lives and the preparation of the baby's room, and then you sit back and wait. Time seems to go by so slowly. You rock back and forth in a new rocking chair that you've just set up in the baby's room; a room prepared just for this new life. Your tummy has stretched and grown and you feel the unknown baby kicking as you gently caress this huge belly with such a tiny form in it. You spend the morning wrapped up in thought about nurturing this little one, feeding it, bathing it, teaching it to walk, and you begin to sing "Jesus Loves Me" to it, and then you continue to wait some more!

The thoughts of 'do I want a boy or a girl' rush through the dads mind. Will it be a boy that walks beside me as I mow, or will he be the opposite of me? Will he enjoy painting, or photography? Will this one be a girl who smiles and giggles, thinks her daddy is Prince Charming and is as beautiful as her mother is? Will she spend constant time putting way too many ribbons and adornments in her hair? Will she change her outfits five times in one afternoon? Will she have a love for shoes that she won't have enough room for in her closet like her mother? Will she draw stick figures of our family with crayon on the wall above her pillow? Then one day you're shopping in the mall or just going about your normal everyday business and your beautiful bride looks up in surprise and embarrassment as her water breaks.

Then you break all speed records rushing to the hospital so that you don't have to deliver the baby in the middle of the mall or in the back of your new car. You are suddenly rushed down the hallway of the local emergency room and into the hospital delivery room and strangers with blue hats and booties get to see you in all your glorious nakedness and start tell you forcibly what to do, things like, 'push!' You cry out, 'Who are you? And where is MY doctor?' Where is my husband who got me into all this mess!" and 'I am pushing!' Finally, after many difficult pushes and several moments of brief rest, and them telling you how to breathe through it all you hear "Okay, now big breath in... let it out, Big breath in... let it out" And just when you start feeling like you have a little bit of relief they tell you, push all over again!

Sound familiar ladies? When you give birth, there is no modesty right? You are there for the whole world to see; you give up trying to cover up. At first, you're walking in to the delivery room they assigned to you and you're covering up stuff, but in the end, when it's birthing time, you don't care what's falling out of that little hospital gown they gave you to wear. You start yelling, 'I want to get this thing out of me! I don't care!' In the meantime your husband finally wanders his way back and finds your room only because he was able to follow the sounds of your screaming voice down the opposite hallway.

When he sees you, it finally dawns on him that he had better get beside you and start practicing all the coaching techniques that he learned to help you in the weeks of birthing class he reluctantly attended. Now you've got your husband there beside you trying to comfort you the best he knows how, and you've got a death grip on him. Men, you never realized just how strong your wives were until then did you? You start thinking to yourself "Oh Lord Jesus, help me, she could take me out at any moment." You say to her, "Oh honey, it'll be alright – everything will be just fine...."

And she yells back at you in almost a very deep and disturbing voice that you have never quite heard come out of her before, "Grrr...I don't like you right now!"

She then squeezes harder and you say "AHHHHH! Oh, thank God, it's almost over!" Then after it's done, and the pressure is gone, and the pain has ended, you both give a huge sigh of relief. Then before you know it, you have given birth to your destiny. After all this time you have finally heard the wonderful crying sound, "Wahhh," and instantly you know what your purpose was. You both hear the baby and your wife sweetly says, "Oh honey I love you so much."

You're thinking – "who are YOU and what did you do with my evil wife?" This child that you just gave birth to was your future, your destiny, your purpose, and God's plan for your life. When you finally hear that sound, Wahhh, you knew what your purpose was in being pregnant. All the thoughts, dreams, and imaginations; all the miserable nausea, cravings, heartburn, never being able to get comfortable, and delivery pains have ended and reality is here. After nine long months and all the incredible changes you went through in the processes you finally gave birth to that wonderful thing that was growing on the inside of you. You not only birthed forth your destiny but God used you and your husband to create another destiny.

I have no idea as a man how painful it must be to give birth other than when I suffered with those kidney stones, (I know, no comparison...)

You begin to push and bear down; you say to yourself, and everyone else, I can't do this, anymore, really, I can't do this. Drugs! Give me drugs! As I was doing my intense study on child bearing for this book I just don't know how some of these women who give birth naturally do it without drugs!

I just have to ask, "What are you all thinking?"

When that baby comes out, you feel joy and release; it's your reward; you can say: "this is my baby, I bore this child, this baby grew on the inside of me. I carried and nurtured it, I sang to it, I prayed for it, I dreamt about it, and I thought about what he or she would look like. I felt every facet of this pregnancy. I felt it kick and move, I could feel the shape of it inside my tummy, I suffered with it, I was in agony with it, and I pushed through it.' When you hear the baby's first cry, it becomes like a dream. It is now a faint memory of nine long months gone by; it becomes your reward! It's then, of course, we men come along and take ownership of it all don't we? We say, "Hey, good job honey! Where's my kid? That's my son; look at him, he looks just like me, doesn't he?" "Wow, we sure went through a lot together, didn't we son?" Mommy is listening and saying to herself, 'oh, brother, give me a break!' While some people just talk and fantasize about their dreams, others are truly fulfilling them by making themselves available to become impregnated by the Holy Spirit with destiny in the spiritual womb of their lives. Divine dreams determine destinies. Dreams and visions are God's destiny forming language. Without them, we become aimless soldiers void of rank, regiment and mission. Divine callings can be birthed by dreams. Those dream seeds swim upstream in the spiritual faith canal of your life and find a place to implant themselves. Visions manifest as a deep desire to serve in a certain area or function in a particular gift or anointing. It is imperative that every believer progressively uncover their calling and mission, or else the cares and distractions of this life will throw us off our divine course into the devil's ditch.

> "Where there is no vision, the people cast off restraint."
>
> Proverbs 29:18

A keen sense of our divine destiny and heavenly calling bridles us from the distractions of life, keeping us trained, and on the race set before us. Like a race horse with blinders, prophetic vision shields us from hindering influences, keeping our focus upon the mark for the prize of attaining our heavenly calling in Christ Jesus. One example of divine destiny being birthed by a prophetic dream and pursued until fulfillment was the life of Joseph (see Genesis 37:5-10). However, the road to his destiny in God was not a smooth one, but instead paved with pitfalls and stumbling blocks. The word of the Lord that Joseph received concerning his life's purpose and destiny (heavenly calling) severely tested him, as he endured the hardship of the pit and the prison before reaching his destiny in the palace.

> "He sent a man before them - Joseph - who was sold as a slave. They hurt his feet with fetters, he was laid in irons. Until the time that his word came to pass, the word of the Lord tested him." (Psalm 105:17-19)

Like Joseph, there are three major variables in every one of our lives; that seem either to assist us or hinder us from reaching our divine purpose and destiny. The first variable is people. Divine destinies always impact other people's lives, and the highway to our purpose and destiny will always be paved with the positive and negative input of others. People and relationships often change like the weather. Oftentimes, when we seek out and need encouragement through a friend, spouse, or parent, instead we find the searing, scorching rays of accusation or disapproval. In the life of Joseph, we find a young man who was rejected, betrayed and sold into slavery by his brothers. Later he was falsely accused of attempted rape by a lustful, lying woman, resulting in an undeserved and extended imprisonment term. Problem people will always seem to detour us from the perfect path to our divine destiny.

The second major variable in life is circumstances. We all like to plan and chart out our course in life to reach our goal, yet many times, we encounter the unexpected that seems to roadblock our journey. Contrary circumstances, as in Joseph's life, often speak death into our destiny.

The third major variable in life is ourselves. We must realize that problem people and contrary circumstances may alter our course in life, but we chiefly determine if we reach our ultimate destination in God. Many times our hindrance is not from other people or outward circumstances it is from our own worst enemy – ourselves! We need to stop and examine Joseph's personality type. What kind of person could endure so much and yet not break? What made Joseph different?

Imagine yourself in a camp at the base of a mountain along with hundreds of other mountain climbers, everyone is starting out with the same goal: to climb the mountain. Each person in the camp is given the same opportunity, the same basic equipment and an equal chance to accomplish the goal, but time shows us that there are three types of people in the camp. They are: "The Can't Doers," The "Campers," and "The Climbers."

The can't doers start at the base of the mountain with everyone else, but they never even attempt the climb. They give up before the journey begins. They never do anything with their lives and constantly make excuses about why they shouldn't try to accomplish anything. If their dad was poor, they figure they will be poor. If Mama had diabetes, they figure they'll have diabetes. They don't trust God enough to believe that they can do all things through Christ who strengthens them, so they stay at the base of the mountain, too fearful to step out.

"The campers" begin climbing the mountain but as soon as adversity comes their way or things don't go quite the way they planned, they sit down and settle for second best. Yes, they attempt the climb, but they don't have the faith to hang in, press through and taste the goodness of God. These are the people who will go out of their way to hold you back. They yell constantly at the folks up ahead explaining why it can't be done, and although they've had a taste of the goodness and an idea of what they are missing, they are too fearful to continue the climb.

"The Climbers" start out at the base of the hill with everyone else, but they are determined to make it to the top. They find strength in adversity and desire to fully taste the goodness of God. If the wind blows cold and hard, they button up and keep on moving. If rocks fall about them, they duck their heads and keep on climbing. They keep pressing, pursuing and they keep praising. They seek the presence of God, and they are determined to be all that He said they would be, and they will have all He promised they would have. They refuse to hear negative reports and choose to keep their eyes fixed on Jesus. If you want to be part of this group, you'll have to face not only Satan and every devil who comes against you but also the "can't doers" and the "campers" as well.

Joseph was a climber; no matter what the enemy threw at him, he caught it and turned it into a touchdown. Even when he was in prison, he managed to turn lemons into lemonade. One night the butler and the baker, who had been imprisoned by Pharaoh, each had dreams. Joseph interpreted their dreams and asked to be remembered when good fortune hit. Though the baker was hanged, the chief butler was restored, just as Joseph had predicted (see Genesis 40:5-22). For a while, the butler forgot about Joseph, but when Pharaoh had a dream, the butler remembered the help he had received from Joseph and told Pharaoh about it (see Genesis 41:9-13). Joseph was summoned to Pharaoh's court, and Pharaoh was so pleased with his interpretations of the dream that he put his own signet ring upon Joseph's hand, arrayed him in fine garments, put gold chains around his neck and made him ride in his second chariot.

In time, Joseph was given an opportunity to seek revenge on his brothers, who had been the source of much pain in his life. However, he chose instead to walk in integrity and honor before God, and to bless and do good before all men. He recognized that his whole life had been in God's hands and that it was God who had sent him to Egypt and preserved his life to be a blessing to His people in a time of famine. When his brothers came to him for food, he told them, "But, as for you, you meant evil against me; but God meant it for good, in order to bring it about as it is this day, to save many people alive." (Genesis 50:20)

What kind of climber are you? Even if you have been a "can't-doer" or a "camper" in the past, it is possible to become a "climber." You just have to move from sitting at the base of the mountain and begin heading toward the top. Do you know God's purpose for your life? Learn to unleash the power of the Holy Spirit and unlock the chains that hinder you from receiving the gifts God has for you. Understand that the enemy will try to abort your dreams. He comes to steal, kill and destroy, but he has no power in your life. Your worship, praise, prayer and obedience can block the enemy from controlling your destiny. Acknowledge that there is a process you must go through. You cannot get from the bottom of the mountain to the top without the climb. The process, the trials and the tests qualify you for the promise. Know that you can endure; your strength comes from Him who is within you. Ask Him for what you need, and He will give it to you, and remember, don't give up! If you set your sights on the mountaintop, He will make certain you get there. When we cease to realize that our dreams and destinies belong to God, and that He is faithful to bring them to pass, the dream has the potential of becoming a god in our lives. Our devotion to a dream, goal or destiny must never supersede our devotion and worship of God. When we cease to pursue the presence of the King and instead labor in vain to fulfill our dream, we invariably exchange His peace and rest for strife, frustration and emptiness.

Oftentimes, dreams become idols in the hearts of those who are driven to pursue them at the expense of everything else, including their family. When problem people and contrary circumstances seem to interfere with our destiny, we often become bitter, blaming others and accusing people of holding us back. However, we must understand that the afflictions and suffering we endure along the way is God's hand perfecting, maturing and equipping us that we may function in our high calling and reach our destiny.

> "May the God of all grace, who called us to His eternal glory by Christ Jesus, after you have suffered a while, perfect, establish, strengthen, and settle you."
>
> I Peter 5:10

Our ways and thoughts are not often those of God. His ways are higher than our ways. Many times, we have a preconceived notion of how God is going to bring about His plan for our lives, and when it doesn't unfold that way, we pout, and we get upset and angry with Him.

> "A man's heart plans his way, but the Lord directs his steps." (Proverbs 16:9)

At this point we reach a crossroads in life where we must do four things before we can continue on the path of life toward our destiny. First, we must die to our dream by surrendering it into God's hands. We, like Abraham, must offer our 'Isaacs' back to the Father. We need to let go and let God. Secondly, we must forgive the problem people in our life that have hurt us and hindered us from reaching our destiny. Joseph forgave a multitude of people, including his brothers, realizing that it was God who worked all things together for good (see Genesis 50:20, 21). Thirdly, we must forget circumstances that have contributed to our failures, resolving to never live in the past by making excuses for our present condition (see Philippians 3:13). Fourthly, we must commit our course to King Jesus, our heavenly Navigator. "Therefore let those who suffer according to the will of God commit their souls to Him in doing good, as to a faithful Creator." (I Peter 4:19).

Despite the many variables of life, we serve an invariable God. He changes not (see Malachi 3:6; James 1:17). He is the same yesterday, today and forever (see Hebrews 13:8). Not only is God's character unchangeable, but His plans, purposes, and destinies upon His children are also irrevocable.

> "For the gifts and the calling of God are without repentance." (Romans 11:29)

Before Jeremiah was formed in His mother's womb, the Lord had called and appointed him a prophet to the nations. (see Jeremiah 1:4, 5). However, we must realize that not only prophets and ministers are called, but every person has a mission. The Bible tells us that the Lord planned each of our lives before He formed the earth and He called us by name, and placed a holy calling upon our lives; a mission for us to fulfill.

> "God has saved us and called us with a holy calling, not according to our works, but according to His own purpose and grace which was given to us in Christ Jesus before time began." (II Timothy 1:9)

No matter what circumstances surrounded our birth, we must realize that the Father planned and had a purpose for our lives before time began. God does not birth mistakes! It is now up to us as individuals to cease from our vain labor and take His yoke upon us. The Lord's light burden and easy yoke are the sacrifice of praise and our labor to continue in the rest of His presence. For it is only in His presence and through His living Word that we will be filled with wisdom and we will be empowered with the weapons necessary to defeat the enemies blocking the path to our Promised Land. It is sobering to realize that our heavenly reward will not be based on our noble achievements and humanitarian efforts, but weighed against our purpose and destiny within His calling. We will be rewarded according to the works He ordained for us, and not our own. Our own works will be burned up at the judgment seat. Those things that we deemed so important, that we spent hours of devotion to, may not be important to Him at all. That which is highly esteemed in man's eyes is often lightly esteemed in God's eyes. The hidden and insignificant labors devoted to the Lord will yield the greater rewards in heaven. Sacrificial works, clothed in the humility of Christ and performed out of obedience to the Master's voice, will bring the greatest rewards.

> "Each one's work will become manifest; for the Day will declare it, because it will be revealed by fire; and the fire will test each one's work, of what sort it is. If anyone's work which he has built on it endures, he will receive a reward. If anyone's work is burned, he will suffer loss; but he himself will be saved, yet so as through fire." (I Corinthians 3:13-15)

In this hour we must determine to walk worthy of the calling with which we have been called, making sure we are walking in the character of Jesus (see Ephesians 4:1,2; II Peter 1:2-11). As we seek the presence of the Lord in all we say and do, we will be transformed into His likeness and prepared for the gifts, calling and anointing He has destined for us. Are we ready, willing, and able to be all that God has intended for us to be in our true purpose and destiny? In the spirit of Joshua and Caleb, we must not only know that we are well able in Christ to conquer the giants that threaten our promises and our well being, but we must be willing to enter that battle boldly as they did. What about you? Are you willing to cross over the Jordan into your Canaan land and be a part of the army of the Lord? I want to declare to you today that you can trust God to bring His plans and purposes to pass in your life. You can trust Him to fulfill the promises He has made to you just as long as you don't settle for anything less than His very best! Even if you don't really know what those promises are right now, just know that God has a divine plan and purpose for your life and He is longing to reveal it to you.

The Fear of The Lord

The Bible says in Psalms 111:10; "The fear of the LORD is the beginning of wisdom."

To fear the Lord is to earnestly respect Him, rising up early and spending time with Him, worshiping and being in His presence, hearing and doing what He says, accepting His plan for your life on His terms. Simply put, the fear of the Lord in a spiritual sense is obedience and compliance to God's agenda for your purpose and destiny. Vision brings passion, passion reveals your purpose, and your purpose releases the power, which brings about your ultimate God ordained destiny. When we operate in a true fear of the Lord, there is a oneness that is created between us and God that unites God's purpose and power in our life. That's the place where we touch true God breathed, God inspired destiny; you know... the type that changes circumstances, people's lives, and moves us into the presence and power of God. True fear of the Lord establishes and releases the authority of God in us. The prophet Hosea says, "My people are destroyed for lack of knowledge." Perhaps it could be said a bit differently: God's people perish for a lack of knowledge of the spiritual authority and purpose God desires us to walk in. Give your vision time; God will give you revelation and clarity as you need it. Each step of your obedience will open up new dimensions and new understandings of God's purposes for your life.

What promise has God proclaimed to you? Is it the restoration of your family? Is it an effective ministry that mends the brokenhearted and touches the city? Maybe a business that is blessed and prospers not only you and your family, but also the Church? Do not settle for anything less than what God has spoken and promised you. The Bible tells us in Numbers 23:19 that, "God is not a man, that He should lie, nor a son of man, that He should repent. Has He not said, and will He not do? Or has He spoken, and will He not make it good?" Child of God, if He said it, you can be sure that He will bring it to pass! You see, the Spirit of God is not content to flutter around on the surface of things, but He likes to dive into the deep things of God. This is the first vital key to being able to discover your purpose and destiny. The Spirit of God searches out and reveals God's plans to man. This is the only way that we can truly fulfill our destiny in life. It is the Spirit of God that leads us into all truth so we must ask the Holy Spirit to reveal God's purpose and destiny to us. Jesus had a lot to say about the Holy Spirit during His earthly ministry.

> "I still have many things to say to you, but you cannot bear them now. "However, when He, the Spirit of truth, has come, He will guide you into all truth; for He will not speak on His own authority, but whatever He hears He will speak; and He will tell you things to come. "He will glorify Me, for He will take of what is Mine and declare it to you. "All things that the Father has are Mine. Therefore I said that He will take of Mine and declare it to you. (John 16:12-15)

The Holy Spirit can take you by the hand and guide you into all the truth. He can help you make sense of what has happened in your life in the past and what is about to happen in the future. He (the Holy Spirit) will take and deliver unto you what God wants to impregnate you with in the spiritual womb of your life. However, as with natural pregnancy is, that which we have been impregnated with in the Spirit is not revealed unto us until the 'due date.' As your purpose is birthed by the Power of the Holy Spirit in the heavenly realm you can then begin to manifest your purpose and destiny in the earthly realm. His Kingdom will come and His will be done on earth, in your life, as it is in heaven.

> "Your kingdom come, Your will be done, on earth as it is in heaven." (Matthew 6:10)

When this kind of thing begins to stir in a believers life it's like how a baby grows on the inside of their mother for a long season until that 'exact moment in time' comes forth for that baby to be birthed. The mother's purpose is fulfilled in the destiny of giving birth to her child. After the travail and that baby breaks forth from its mother's womb into the world that baby takes its very first breath of air and cries out with a loud voice! One purpose and destiny comes to a close (the mother's purpose for giving birth) and another purpose and destiny now begins for the newborn baby to discover its own unique God ordained reason for existence on earth.

Chapter 9
Impregnated With Purpose

Many of you reading this book have already been impregnated in the spiritual womb of your life by the divine Seed of heaven. The kingdom is coming on earth as it is in heaven. The Lord wants to bring down those things that are in the heavenly realm, the things that are foreseen. He wants those things that have been known about you since the beginning of the creation of the world to be brought down and implanted into our hearts and minds. He desires to begin to impart those divine spiritual things that are locked up in the heavenly realms to those of us who are passionately seeking Him for our purpose and destiny in Christ in the earthly realm. He wants to birth them and manifest them through each of our lives, to bring His kingdom on the earth and to see His will being done in the earth until He comes again. Ladies, the Bible tells us that the fruit of your womb is a heritage from the Lord. In Psalm 127:3 we read, "Behold, children are a heritage from the Lord..." Listen; no matter how much they are driving you nuts right now, they are a heritage and a blessing from the Lord. No matter how much anxiety or stress they're giving you, or how many added gray hairs upon your head, children are a heritage from the Lord. The fruit of the womb is a reward!

When God allowed the seed of a man to be planted within you and it impregnated you, it was part of the Adamic blessing of multiplication. God told Adam and Eve to be fruitful and multiply and to fill the earth. Being fruitful and multiply simply meant to procreate and bring forth children from the fruit of a woman's womb to fill the earth with divine destinies that will take dominion, rule, and subdue the earth in His divine purposes.

There are people who are filled with purpose, passion, and with a desire to subdue and take dominion and do something great for the Lord! There are people who have said, "Lord, here is my spiritual womb; impregnate me that I might bring forth your purposes on the earth." As a new believer in Jesus Christ, many of you have just recently been impregnated spiritually. In fact, there are some who have just recently come back to the Lord after being away from Him for a long period of time, and they are on fire for God! They are at the church whenever the doors are open and stay until the doors are closed. Whenever there is something going on, they are first in line because deep down in their inner man they know they are going to give birth to something great. They truly have been impregnated in the spiritual womb of their life with a sense of purpose and destiny.

There are apostles, prophets, evangelists, pastors and teachers just waiting to be birthed, the five-fold ministry gifts. You've been impregnated with something; you've had the divine Seed of heaven implanted inside the spiritual womb of your life. As he did with Mary, the Holy Spirit has overshadowed you and you have become pregnant with Heavens plans and purpose for your life. Some of you your deepest hearts cry has been "God, use me!" Some of you are pastors and ministry leaders already, but you are not quite where you want to be yet. God is about ready to birth and bring forth your ultimate purpose and destiny. You are truly getting ready to find out why you are here on this earth, why you live and move and have your being, why you breathe the way you breathe, and why your heart beats the way it beats. When you sleep, you arise because of your purpose and destiny. When you arise, you live every day to walk out your purpose and destiny.

There are others that are already pregnant with purpose and vision. Hallelujah! You know who you are. You are the ones in full-time ministry, and maybe a pastor of a growing church, but there are many things that come along with that and many things that seem to get in the way of truly giving birth to and manifesting your life's purpose and destiny. You are possibly married, maybe you have children, you have spiritual children, and your personal schedule, ministry, and travel schedules are so full with all of these busy things to do. I pray you will obtain the necessary instructions and the information you need to continue to breathe and to push through your time of spiritual labor pains so that you'll be able to see your promised seed, your true purpose and destiny from God materialize and come to pass before your very eyes.

As in the natural birthing process when a woman has just given birth to a precious life, she wants to hold and behold her miracle. I pray that your miracle will be something wonderful and magnificent for you to behold. I pray that as you continue to push through the many distractions to your purpose and destiny that in time your promised miracle will be fully manifested and birthed before your eyes as well. Praise God! Did you know that as a believer you are part of the church? The Bible declares that we (all believers both male and female) are the Bride of Christ. We are all part of the body of Christ and that makes us the church, His soon to be Bride. The body of Christ is characterized as feminine in the Bible. We are the bride being prepared for our Bridegroom, Jesus Christ the Lamb of God. He is coming back for a Holy bride without spot or wrinkle.

> "Husbands, love your wives, just as Christ also loved the church and gave Himself for her, that He might sanctify and

> cleanse her with the washing of water by the word, that He might present her to Himself a glorious church, not having spot or wrinkle or any such thing, but that she should be holy and without blemish."
>
> Ephesians 5:25-27
>
> "Then I, John, saw the holy city, New Jerusalem, coming down out of heaven from God, prepared as a bride adorned for her husband. And I heard a loud voice from heaven saying, "Behold, the tabernacle of God is with men, and He will dwell with them, and they shall be His people. God Himself will be with them and be their God." (Revelation 21:2-3)

So men, even for you there's a feminine side to you that you need to learn about now in a healthy way. I'm not talking about in the worldly perverted way, or the way that the enemy would like certain men to believe. I'm not talking about the femininity that is promoted in the world through homosexuality; I'm talking about something spiritual, Godly, and holy here. Men need to embrace and understand that they are feminine in a biblical and Godly connotation, in the sense that we are all part of the Bride of Christ, every one of us, both men and women. We are going to be a great and glorious bride someday, and Jesus our Bridegroom will come back and unite Himself with us, His beautiful bride. What a glorious day that will be.

My Miracle Birth

Let me tell you the story of my miracle birth. My precious mother Racheal was pregnant with me and the due date for my purpose and destiny to be born in the earth was January 28, 1965. My mother was just 20 years old when she gave birth to me. She had problems throughout her entire pregnancy and began to go through the process of labor and delivery. How many know the devil is a liar and will try to abort anyone's destiny in whom he thinks will become a threat to him and to the kingdom of darkness in any way shape or form? The devil has understanding of these things. He was in the heavenly dimension before he was thrown out of heaven and into the lower earthly dimension. The Bible says that he was an anointed heavenly cherub and was in charge of all the worship around the throne.

> ."..You were the seal of perfection, Full of wisdom and perfect in beauty. You were in Eden, the garden of God; Every precious stone was your covering: The sardius, topaz, and diamond, Beryl, onyx, and jasper, Sapphire, turquoise, and emerald with gold. The workmanship of your timbrels and pipes was prepared for you on the day you were created. "You were the anointed cherub who covers; I established you; You were on the holy mountain of God; You walked back and forth in the midst of fiery stones. You were perfect in your ways from the day you were created, till iniquity was found in you. "By the abundance of your trading You became filled with violence within, And you sinned; Therefore I cast you as a profane thing Out of the mountain of God." (Ezekiel 28:13-16)

The Bible also goes on to describe how he was cast out of heaven:

> And He (Jesus) said to them, "I saw Satan fall like lightning from heaven." (Luke 10:18)

> "And war broke out in heaven: Michael and his angels fought with the dragon; and the dragon and his angels fought, but they did not prevail, nor was a place found for them in heaven any longer. So the great dragon was cast out, that serpent of old, called the Devil and Satan, who deceives the whole world; he was cast to the earth, and his angels were cast out

> with him. Then I heard a loud voice saying in heaven, "Now salvation, and strength, and the kingdom of our God, and the power of His Christ have come, for the accuser of our brethren, who accused them before our God day and night, has been cast down. (Revelation 12:7-10)

Now, let's not get hung up theologically on this part. Some people believe certain things about the second and third heaven and all sorts of other opinions when it comes to where the devil has been cast down to and where he has set up his demonic headquarters now. All I'm saying is that the devil has been cast down out of heaven and is now a part of another lower realm. He is more familiar with the earthly realm now, but he still has a memory of those things that he knew as an anointed cherub in the heavenly dimension. So he understands certain divine principles and how they operate in the heavenly realms and now tries to deceive and confuse the sons of men so they will not be able to fulfill their divine purpose and destiny.

Back to the story of my miracle birth, he (the devil) began to lie to my mother and say that her first-born wouldn't make it. This is how Satan operates. He tries to torment us with lies over and over again to get us to agree with his demonic plans and intentions for us so we won't believe God's true and divine purpose for our lives.

In a very intense and critical medical situation my mother went into labor. The story goes when she began to give birth to me as I came out, I took my first breath of life too soon and I breathed in the amniotic fluid that I had just been swimming in moments before. Needless to say, my tiny lungs filled up and I couldn't breathe. The doctors and the nurses were working frantically to rescue me but I continued to struggle, and still I could not breathe. My mother was asking about me, "How's my baby? Why isn't he crying or making any noise?"

Of course the doctors and nurses aren't going to tell you until they hear the baby cry out and they know that the heart and lungs are working properly. They knew what was happening to me, but they only told her that everything was going to be okay. They continued to work on me for a while but as time went on, I became very critical.

Back in those days they didn't have all the technology they have now. The doctor didn't quite know what to do anymore, nothing seemed to be working to get me to breathe. The nurses didn't know what to do either, but God knew what to do for me because He had a reason for placing me inside my mother's womb, and He had a divine purpose and reason for me to be born at that exact moment in time in the earth. It was then that God decided to step in and intervene by divine revelation.

How many know that God knows just when to send divine intervention? He knows when and how to send a message to the earthly realm to accomplish His plans and purposes in the earth. He knows just when to break through and bring forth divine revelation knowledge, and that's what He did. God spoke the plan out of heaven and placed this plan into the doctor's mind and heart.

Right in the middle of all this confusion, the doctor said "give me the baby!" He wrapped me in blankets, ran out of the delivery room, down the hospital hallway all the way outside the building, ran up to a water spigot. He turned it on and placed me under the thing and the rush of cold water began to hit my little face and all of a sudden he heard me take a great big gasp of air and I cried out "Wahhhh!"

I don't know anything more about this doctor. I don't know if he was Jewish, Christian, Islamic, or an atheist for that matter. I don't know where he stood with the things of God. I only know that God brought a divine revelation into that delivery room that day and God spoke the answer that doctor needed to save my natural life and to preserve my life's purpose and destiny! God had a purpose for my life. I was that close to not making it, but God had a purpose and a plan for me. God had a destiny for me to fulfill, and now I tell people that I got baptized at birth. Hallelujah, I was baptized underneath a water spigot! Why was I baptized at birth? Very simple, God had a plan for me! He planned that I would be born in that moment, on that day, for a very specific reason. The same is true of you and your birth. God has a very unique plan and purpose for you to fulfill in the earth.

Chapter 10
God Wants You!

Every one of us was born for a reason. I don't know what surrounded the events of your birth, if your parents were precious loving caring parents like mine or not. I don't know if you had a stable home environment or just the opposite. I don't know if your parents wanted you or if they didn't want you, if they were married and pre-planned you or if you were considered an oops and they never planned to have a new baby enter their lives. I don't know what your environment was like, but it doesn't matter, because God wanted you and you are here for a purpose.

Maybe you were born then given up for adoption? It doesn't matter, because God wanted you, and that is why you were birthed out of your mother's womb from her egg and from your father's sperm. The two met by heavens design and you started living inside of your mother's womb. There was a reason for you to be birthed! You are not a mistake no matter what was said to you in fun or in haste by your birth mother or father. You are not a mistake. You are here by divine appointment for a redemptive purpose.

Maybe you are someone who wonders why you were ever born. God is going to give you hope and a promise for your life. Hear me: It's just beginning for you. You're just getting started with the best times of your life. Why? Simply put, there is a reason and a meaning for your life. There is a perfect plan for your life. The Lord is just waiting to reveal what His plan is for you in Jesus Christ. The Creator of the universe wants you to uncover His unique, redemptive plan and purpose for your life. Listen to this: the God of Abraham, Isaac, and Jacob wants to reveal Himself to you in a way that you never dreamed possible. He wants to give you true meaning and purpose for why you were born into this world, and why you are here on planet earth.

I believe that nothing happens by accident, but all things are divinely orchestrated and created by God, to help us understand the true meaning and purpose for our life. Listen to me, God does not waste anything. Everything that you've ever gone through in life thus far has been for a purpose.

You say, "Pastor Brian, even the bad things, the horrible things I did when I was a prodigal son or daughter living for myself in the world? When I was lying in the gutter, when I was on drugs, when I was an alcoholic?" YES! The Bible says in Romans 11:29, "...for the gifts and calling of God are without repentance." God doesn't waste anything, He'll use it all. Oh Hallelujah!

You say, "How could God use all that for good in my life?" He was revealing things to you all through that time. He was trying to show you that your purpose wasn't to be where you were at the moment. It was to be where you need to be, and where you're going to be, and who you are today. He wants to show you what was established in the heavenly realm and planned for you from the foundations of the earth. As a little boy I knew, even way back then, that there was something different about my life. The Lord just seemed to give me a special discernment inside of me that something was different about my life.

I wasn't going to be like everyone else. I just knew it. I thought to myself many times that I was different from my peers and family members. Something was different inside and I couldn't really explain it to anyone other than I knew that I would be doing something very special with my life. I mean I did everything that everyone else did, I did all the sports, all the kid stuff, and all the teen stuff, and I had a good time doing it. I was good at it and I loved it, but at the end of the day on my bed at night, I would ponder to myself about what it was that felt so different. It seemed like what fueled other people only fueled me for a little while, but then nothing.

I remember as a young boy I would go outside our home at night and get up on my parent's vehicle and lay down on the hood and I would look up into the night sky, or into the clouds on a late afternoon, and I would wonder about what was up there. I would wonder if there really was a God who made all this. Maybe it happened for you a different way, but like me, many of you did similar things and maybe still wonder who you are in the vastness of humanity.

Well, I can tell you for certain and with conviction that God truly does have a purpose and a plan for every one of you. You have got to get back to this basic understanding of life so you can live it out with true purpose. You know, there is such a huge emphasis right now about purpose. All kinds of books (including this one) are being published marketed and distributed to thousands. Why is that? Because there is a demand for them. People are hungry to know what their true life's purpose and destiny is and they are saying to themselves and maybe to others that there has got to be more to life than what they have experienced thus far.

God desires to help us understand that we have a purpose and we all have a destiny. You cannot have a destiny without purpose, nor can you have purpose without a destiny. When you have purpose, you have passion. When I finally discovered my purpose, when I finally figured out what I was supposed to do in the Kingdom, I got passionate and things began to happen. The purpose was there, but I had to get passionate about it and start moving in that direction. When I had passion I had greater purpose, and my passion to do my purpose became the vehicle that drove me to fulfill my destiny of preaching and teaching.

What is your passion in life? Could it be a clue as to what your greater purpose in life is? I think so. Many times people get confused and become disillusioned or frustrated. Maybe you didn't feel the same sense of discernment that I did when I was growing up. Yet you still really want to know what your path is and what choices will bring you success, but it seems as if you keep hitting a block wall. You search for that answer in so many places and some of you just collapse and become angry at life and at yourself. You ask yourself "why do so many act like they're content and I just keep going around in circles? I never feel satisfied. I'm a failure."

As I stated before, I spent almost six years in the behavioral health field before I went full time in ministry. Believe me, I've seen a lot of stuff, and heard it all as well. I've counseled a lot of people and assessed them with major problems. There are a lot of people that have no clue and no idea what they are here for. They spend their whole lives running here, running there, and trying this and trying that. They are looking desperately to find their purpose. They try so many "other things" before they decide to come to God and none of these things can satisfy them.

Some of you remember the days of trying this drug and trying that drink and testing out that relationship, trying this career and then that career, trying to make the big money, buying the large house, and this toy, and that toy, the fancy car, etc. Then you get those things and you still feel empty and void inside. You thought you would feel something that said you had arrived and all you felt was this overwhelming sense of futility, so you try harder, you push harder, and you stay up longer at night. You can't sleep because of all the stuff that you've acquired that you can't even pay for now. You try to run here and there to medicate yourself and fill the emptiness and void. You have this failed marriage and then try that marriage, and the next one. Without God and without the Holy Spirit leading, directing, and guiding you every step and at every juncture of your destiny then life is left to fate. Fate is the opposite of faith, it is governed by chance. That's a scary place to build your life, but faith is built on God's Word and His promises. God's promises are sure and true with predetermined successful outcomes and results.

As all births go, you just can't go right from conception to giving birth. There is a season of preparation. The normal season is nine months. Nine is a very powerful Biblical number. Interestingly enough the number nine represents the fruit of the womb, the fruit of the spirit, and the nine gifts of the spirit. Eight is the biblical number for new beginnings and newness of life. So when you move from eight to nine it represents the fruit of new life. That's when all of those new beginnings culminate into tangible fruit. In Genesis, God gave Adam and Eve a purpose. He said, "Be fruitful and multiply; fill the earth...." (Genesis 1:28) How do you do that? You have relationship, and intimacy, and from that, you bear the fruit of children. Your womb becomes fruitful and you multiply. Ladies, some of you did a good job at fulfilling that scripture verse, therefore you are a modern day Eve. You are continuing to obey and fulfill God's command to be fruitful and multiply. For others maybe you are right in the beginning stages of pregnancy. Maybe you just heard you are pregnant and you are saying in astonishment "Oh my goodness I'm pregnant! There is a baby beginning to grow on the inside of me!" To that, I say Congratulations!

It can be the same way in the spirit for both men and woman. In the spirit, this incredible experience is not just limited to women. You may be feeling pregnant in the spiritual womb of your life and you can be saying in your soul, "I'm pregnant! I've got to do something for God!"

Maybe you are farther along than you realize, and you're already in the sixth, seventh or eighth month and you're saying, "Oh, God when? When God? I just can't carry this thing anymore!"

If this describes you in any way, either in the natural or the spiritual, then you are in a time of preparation. You see, with natural pregnancy they teach and train you from day one to get ready for the last day. Why? Because you don't want to be unprepared for the day of birth. When you start getting into the latter months, what do you do with pregnancy? You prepare. They tell you and your husband to get a bag together because it may come sooner than you think. There is even a time during the preparation process that things reach a place where it even goes beyond the realm of what medical doctors can predict. In other words, they tell you the month and the approximate day your due date is expected, but it almost never happens on the specified date. So then what do you do?

You wait and wait some more, but what do they tell you to do in the waiting? That's right – prepare, because when its birthing time and your water breaks, and you hear, 'Whoosh' you don't have to guess what just happened to you. Your water broke and as it begins to gush out, in moments it becomes time to give birth. When it's your time to go into labor you had better be ready both naturally and spiritually.

Most of the time women are very calm and we men are the ones frantically saying, "OK, what do we do? I don't know what to do? Tell me what we should be doing!" And all along, everything we needed is right there in front of us. You have the bag, all the numbers, whom you're to call, and whom the other kids are going to stay with. The same is true in your spiritual pregnancy you prepare for the 'whoosh' in God. If the 'whoosh' hasn't come for you yet, don't despise the preparation and the time of waiting.

This is something I did in my spiritual pregnancy. I wanted to go from conception to birthing, and you just can't do that. As in natural pregnancy, it is impossible. You have to go through the process of pregnancy, and all the changes that comes with it. You have to develop, and learn, you definitely have to grow and stretch; you have to go through the process of change just like in natural pregnancy. Ladies, you all know what I'm talking about. You start out in conception looking like the same size you had been before you became pregnant, but just a few short months later you're out looking for larger sizes. Then as the weeks and months go by, you move on from going to the large size department to the plus sizes, and then you finally break down and start perusing the maternity section for all the cute clothes. Try as you may, you cannot remain in the regular sizes due to the process of change that is taking place on the inside of you. You can't stop growing no matter how hard you try.

This is what happens to someone who becomes pregnant with their divine purpose and destiny. They start out looking and feeling the same, but over time as they allow the Holy Spirit to take them through the process of growth and development they begin to stretch spiritually and they develop the capacity to hold the God given destiny that is waiting to be pushed out of them in time. There is just something about pregnant women, I love the glow that pregnant women give off. There is just something so special about it. There is a Biblical reason why pregnant women glow . It was established from the beginning of time that this is how God is going to save the nations. It's through the glow of women.

You see, they give birth to destinies, and that's why God put enmity there in the beginning. Ladies, that's why He gave you so much pain and travail in birth, because one day a woman named Mary would give birth to the Light of the World. Is anyone getting this? So despise not your preparation time. You are in preparation for your purpose, and for your destiny. You were being prepared for God's plan from the first day you burst out of your mother's womb and cried, 'Waahhh!' Thank you, Jesus!

Chapter 11
Jesus Gave Birth To Destiny

Water is very significant biblically. It is a physical form or manifestation of the anointing or presence of God. Jesus went to the Jordan waters to be baptized and He gave birth to His purpose and destiny there (Matthew 3:11). I've actually traveled to Israel many times and have been baptized there and I have also had the honor and the privilege of baptizing many other people in the Jordan River in the Holy Land. It is an amazingly beautiful experience each and every time. In John the Baptists traditional Jewish way, he baptized Jesus in those waters. When Jesus came out of the water He gushed forth, and God's voice came out of heaven, and said, "This is My beloved Son, in whom I am well pleased." (Matthew 3:17)

What happened out of the heavenly dimension? What burst forth from the heavenly realm? A voice came out of the heavens and a beautiful white dove, symbolizing the power of the Holy Spirit, came down, as Jesus came up, it settled and rested upon His shoulder. He, (God) gave birth to His only begotten Son's ministry on earth, and God said, "I am well pleased." He gave birth to Jesus' purpose and destiny for coming! Are you with me? He gave birth! Whoosh! The water broke forth and He came out of those waters prepared for His purpose and ready to carry out His destiny. The voice of God acknowledged His purpose; God the Father acknowledging, "This is My Son!" From that day forward, Jesus' purpose was birthed and He faithfully walked out His destiny to the very end. Why was He here? What was His purpose and destiny? It was to seek and to save the lost, to save the entire world of sin and to give everyone the promise of eternal life.

All throughout the Bible in the Old Testament there are types and shadows revealing the life of Jesus. How I describe this to students in my Bible College is like this: The Old Testament is the New Testament concealed and the New Testament is the Old Testament revealed. In the Old Testament law, the type and shadow was that there had to be a lamb slain for the remission of sin. From Isaiah 53 down through all of the wonderful prophetic messianic passages in the Old Testament, almost all of the types and shadows contained in the Old Testament point to this destiny. They point to the day that Jesus would be hung on the cross for you and me. They pointed to the Son of God giving His life for all of our sins. Oh, Hallelujah! There was a day in the Garden of Gethsemane when Jesus fell on His knees before God in that Garden and said, "O my Father, if it is possible, let this cup pass from me." He then continued, "nevertheless, not as I will, but as You will." (Matthew 26:39)

What cup was Jesus talking about? Well, you see, Jesus knew His purpose and He walked out His destiny even unto death. What lay in wait for Him and His destiny? His destiny was to die on a cross. Why? So He could re-establish some things in the heavenly realm. John said, "And He Himself is the propitiation for our sins, and not for ours only but also for the whole world." (I John 2:2)

Isaiah said, "But He was wounded for our transgressions, He was bruised for our iniquities; the chastisement for our peace was upon

Him, and by His stripes we are healed." (Isaiah 53:5) It was so we could have a Savior; He's the Savior of our soul who died for our sins. It places us in right standing with God, and now He looks upon us as being righteous before him. There was a son named Adam birthed in the book of Genesis who fell short in his divine purpose and destiny, but there was another Son – a Son who followed through and fulfilled His divine destiny. When this Son said, "O my Father, if it is possible, let this cup pass from Me." Right there and then He started feeling the labor pains of His destiny. He got pregnant at the Jordan, He pushed in the Garden, and He gave birth at the cross and saved the entire world, past, present, future for all eternity. Oh, Hallelujah! Aren't you glad Jesus was pregnant with us on the inside of Him? He was giving birth to our salvation and our redemption! He was giving birth to you and I, and He gave His life to do it! See, you don't realize in the preparation time just what God really wants to do until it's time for birthing.

The Seed Brings Forth New Life

I gave my life to Jesus Christ at sixteen years old. That was twenty eight years ago and I am just now beginning to walk in dimensions of my purpose and destiny that I only had visions and dreamt about when I was that young. I have been passionately following hard after the things of God ever since, but where I got messed up the most in my journey was when I wanted to hurry up and push through all the season of preparation. It was the one thing that seemed to mess me up the most. In my hurry, I began to struggle and trip myself up a lot. It was as if I got spiritually pregnant and I miscarried a few times along the way. God's plan is not for us to miscarry our purpose and destiny, but to be fruitful, multiply, and bear fruit. Praise be to God! The moment you realize that it's time to give birth, you know - it's time, Hallelujah! Contractions begin in your life, and in the Spirit you begin to hear the Lord say, "push, now, it's time! Push! Breathe! Push!"

Come on ladies, you know when it's time, and you are on that table in the delivery room, they don't yell out a wimpy push. They yell out, Push! Come on and say it, push! Now breathe, take a breath..., now, from this point forward in the book, whenever you read the word "push," what are you going to do? You are going to declare aloud, "push!" Over your very own purpose and destiny, and then you're going to take a deep breath (literally breathe in) the breath of the Spirit. Here's why, in natural childbirth what seems like an eternity, in all reality, in the grand scheme of time, is just a few very intense moments with deep breaths in between. Ladies, when you were giving birth, it seemed like an eternity didn't it? Some births can last for awhile, and other times it goes rather quickly, but God knows how long you need to push. God knows how much time you need. When the preparation time has reached the pushing time you're ready to give birth to something so big, so great, so powerful, and you feel as if you could never give birth to it on your own, or in your own strength.

But ladies, just like in natural childbearing, somehow, you found the faith, the inner strength, and the power to continue pushing until your promised blessing is finally revealed to you. This is what happens in the Spirit as well. We continue to push and breathe... until our destiny is ready to be birthed. God will give you the faith, inner strength, and the power to continue pushing until your promise is revealed. Some people are given promises from God in their youth, and some may not get their promise until later in life, but either way when that promise is finally birthed and revealed it is a miracle come true. It is finally manifested on the earth. I'll say it again, the vision God wants to impregnate us with is something so wonderful and magnificent! The Bible says that we can't even begin to think or dream about how magnificent it is. Why? God only does magnificent and wonderful things.

> But as it is written: "Eye has not seen, nor ear heard, Nor have entered into the heart of man The things which God

> has prepared for those who love Him." But God has revealed them to us through His Spirit. For the Spirit searches all things, yes, the deep things of God." (I Corinthians 2:9-10)

All you have to do is look around at Creation. When I travel either in the sates or abroad, I love to look at God's wondrous Creation in the earth. Just stop and take a look around you right now, or when you have an opportunity take a fresh new look at the scenery and the topography of the area you live. Whether it's a luscious green area or dry hot area like Arizona, or somewhere in between, our Creator God made it all and it's beautiful! Right now, even as I am writing this book we are in a season in Phoenix, Arizona of absolute beauty. It has rained, and the rain has broken a season of drought in our area. God's blessing has poured down upon us out of heaven and has broken Arizona's barrenness! Now those tiny droplets will penetrate the dry crusty earth and bring forth new life! No matter what people want to believe, God brought forth the much-needed rain and now everything is going to become green with new life. It's beautiful because now the desert is blossoming like a rose, and just like this natural desert, the Lord can turn your spiritual wilderness and your desert into a fruitful field.

> "The wilderness and the wasteland shall be glad for them, and the desert shall rejoice and blossom as the rose; It shall blossom abundantly and rejoice...." (Isaiah 35:1, 2)

I recently took a drive up to the northern part of the state and the riverbeds, and creeks were full of water. It's not just trickling, either, it's really moving. Then you look around and because of the life giving rain the desert has become so beautiful. You can just look at it and see how wonderful the blessing of God has created it to be.

The same is true for you child of God. Just how God's blessing (the rain, the life giving water) penetrated the dry barren earth (your life), and it brought forth new life (your new life in Christ), the Lord wants to impregnate you with something so magnificent that He is the only one that can help you give birth to it (your divine purpose and destiny). The Lord created and deposits what I call dream seeds. Now, from here on out, when you hear me talking about seeds or dream seeds, I'm referring to the masculine side of procreation. I am talking about sperm; no human birth can be created without it. God put that special component (sperm) inside of man and He put eggs inside of women so that they could meet and new life could be created. The sperm in man is life giving. It was first given and placed there by God Himself. Though there are many of them, only one has to hit its mark to create destiny. God uses sperm to fertilize the seed, and causes the seed and the egg to spring forth to create new life, a new purpose and destiny is created and formed.

From the foundations of time, from Genesis through Revelation, the Bible says if you plant a seed, all it takes is one, it will grow! Here again, the natural revealing the spiritual, and the spiritual revealing the natural. Here is the real unique part, once the seed is planted it comes up out of its' own kind. Man has tried to manipulate things in the world and has been somewhat successful in the animal and plant kingdoms, by making certain ones grow the way they want them to, but man always tries to make things bend to fit his will.

God established His will from the foundations of the earth. When a seed is planted, it comes up after its 'own kind.' When a man's seed is planted inside a fertile womb of a woman, the sperm meets the egg, and it comes forth out of its' own kind. Sometimes it's a man and sometimes it's a woman, but either way they were both made in the image and likeness of God. You have what it takes to become all that He has intended for you to be. Don't try and live your life by trying to bend things to your own will, but submit to God's will and allow the life giving waters of His Spirit to rain down upon you (His divine plan and purposes for your life) and bring forth new life!

Chapter 12
The 'Us' Factor

You are made in the image of God, so when you are born it is like the image of God being birthed in the earth. He made us after Himself; He made us in like kind. In Genesis 1:26 it says, "Let Us make man in Our own image; according to Our likeness." In whose image? We were made in the image of the Father, the Son, and the precious Holy Spirit. I don't know what your theology says about the holy Trinity, but I am telling you from Genesis to Revelation, up, down, sideways, forwards and backwards, and in every way possible, it speaks of the Triune nature of God (the Trinity). I like to call the trinity the 'Us factor,' all three persons of the Godhead wrapped up in One. You and I, man and woman, were created like all three Father, Son, and Holy Spirit, and yet we are one person. If you want to understand the Trinity there it is, "Let Us make man in Our own image."

There are three wonderful characteristics of the personalities of the Godhead contained on the inside of you! Think about that for a minute. Each part of the character of the triune nature of God has been placed within us – within our DNA as a man or woman. Let me try to explain in a more practical way if I can.

I can't tell you how many times that other people's nurture and care for me have been like the Holy Spirit in my life. When I have needed a little truth, understanding, love, or some comfort, they have been much like how the Holy Spirit is with me. There are other times in my life where Godly people's nurture and care for me have been much like how Jesus is with me. They love me in spite of me. Hallelujah!

I'm sure that there have been people in your life somewhere along the way (a parent, spouse, child, friend, etc.) who have loved you in spite of you. Those special people who have sacrificed in different ways to show they truly love and care about you. Those people remind me of Jesus' love.

Then there are other times where peoples' nurture and care for me have reminded me of the Father's love; they represent the apostolic, divine order, discipline, government, safety and protection, and just like a caring faithful authoritative father they have challenged me to get my life together. This is a special example of how the triune nature of God is activated inside of us and works through our purpose and destiny. The divine DNA within our human makeup helps us to emulate and look like the very image, likeness, and nature of God. In other words, they see the 'Us factor,' God within us and they don't see the us (lowercase u) in us.

My middle son, Michael David, had a special reward that they gave out at his grade school. When a child is good throughout the course of a day they are given a 'happy gram' that is sent home in their backpacks to indicate to the parents the child's daily progress and behavior. Each child strives to get a "happy gram" because after twenty in a row, they are rewarded for their good behavior with special prizes.

On the other hand, if they are bad throughout the day, after three warnings and the teacher working diligently with the child, with no improvement in their behavior, they give them what's called a "cloudy gram." I am happy to say that Michael has been consistent in bringing home "happy grams" almost every school day. But one day he got is very first "cloudy gram." When Michael got home from school Phaedra asked him as she usually does every day if he had gotten a "happy gram" and Mike said with bit of hesitation and squeamish grin, "Ummm... yeah, I got a happy gram today."

We ask about this every day so it wasn't that Phaedra's prophetic power gifts were in keen operation that day telling us that Michael had been bad all day. Phaedra and I just like to be supportive and we have often used this time to encourage positive behavior with all our kids as this builds their character, integrity, and self esteem. We like to keep in close contact with Michael's teachers because he has struggled in certain areas in school and we desire to help him to succeed in class and with homework. Phaedra then proceeded to ask him again for some strange reason, "Michael, did you say you got a happy gram or a cloudy gram today?" He didn't want to tell us in fear of getting in trouble and getting his privileges taken away. He's just a normal child growing, learning, and changing and testing the boundaries and limits of his parents.

Let me set the scene a little better for you. I had just walked in that evening from a long day at work and my Abigail ran up to greet me as she always does when I come home. It makes every day sweet no matter how good or bad it's been. "Daddy! Daddy's home! Woo-Who!" Michael is sitting there at the homework table kind of nervously rubbing his hands and Abigail is running up on me and jumping up on me to hug my neck to tell me a gazillion things she did that day all in one breath. While this particular day Michael didn't run up to me to give me his hug but remained sitting there at the table and says, "Umm... Hey Dad, I got a happy gram today." Now remember, he knew all along he got a "cloudy gram." So he was working it out in his own mind how he was going to make it through the next couple of days until we talked to his teacher.

Those of you reading this book that have kids know what I'm talking about don't you? He thought, dad responds happily to "happy grams" so I will just ride this lie out as long as I can in order to not have to deal with the consequences of my actions, and as long as they don't know then I'll be alright. Yes, I believe that is what good parents respond to, and it's like how our heavenly Father responds to us. When we're doing right in His eyes, He responds happily to us. It's called 'Righteousness' in the Word of God or being in 'right standing' with Him.

Well, with nervous hands (sometimes Michael rubs his hands together when he is nervous or in trouble) and a silly grin on his face he went through the night thinking he was fooling us, but the next day my wife Phaedra drove Michael to school, got out of the car and walked him up to his classroom. As she walked Michael up to the door to check him into class, the morning bell had already rung, and all of a sudden, as Phaedra was walking back towards her car getting ready to leave, Michael came running back out the door. She is looking at him wondering what in the world is he doing out of class? Then Michael comes swiftly up to her and he says, "Mom, the teacher told me to come out here and give you a hug - yeah... a hug!"

She is thinking, okay? So she hugged him back and then she said, "Michael, you need to get back to class, school has started already." He said, "Well, the teacher told me to come out and give you a hug." So she walked Michael back into to the classroom. One of the helper moms comes out and she says, "Mrs. Alton, did Michael tell you why he came back out here to get you?" She said, "No, he just said that his teacher wanted him to give me a hug." She said, "Um, he got a cloudy gram yesterday and he was suppose to go home and show you yesterday so you could sign the back of it. Now the teacher needs to see you so you can discuss it with her and sign it this morning." Well, needless to say, Michael was, as we say around the Alton home, "busted."

In this case of willful sin, cover up, and lies to us, the punishment was that Michael was going to have to face his father when he got home. In our home, I am the final step in the process of correction. We have been able to instill a healthy and Godly respect for all our children that if mom has to get to the point in her discipline measures of having to say; "Ok, that's it, just wait till your Father gets home" it sends a shockwave through their entire being! It's amazing how they can go from behaving badly to repenting tearfully from all their recent sins and they quickly turn into sweet little obedient children.

Now, I'm going somewhere with this story. You see, my wife, and the teacher were like Jesus and the Holy Spirit to Michael, but he ultimately had to face his father over his willful sin and actions. He knows, if there is one thing that my wife and I despise is lies, because there is a father of all lies and we despise him. Michael's mom dealt with him and she did a wonderful job, but she really didn't think that he was getting it about the lies (he had been testing these boundaries for a few weeks now).

So she said, "Michael, you're going to have to tell Dad why you lied to us. You didn't just lie to me, but you willfully lied to Daddy as well." We were busy with church and ministry stuff that night so we really didn't check as thoroughly as we would have liked to. Are you seeing the parallel here?

Let me tell you something, I had to be the father; I had to be the apostolic piece. You know, I like to play the role of Jesus and the Holy Spirit, meaning being able to show grace and mercy all the time, as I'm sure many of you do too, but sometimes a father figure has to be like the heavenly Father's character, the final authority of grace, mercy, or the authority of correction and final judgment. You see, the Father represents the apostolic anointing. The apostle reproduces, and impregnates, he helps bring divine government, order, and structure to our lives and into the house of God. That's what the job description of a natural healthy father figure is in a family as well.

The father represents divine order. He's the one that holds all things together. Our heavenly Father is the only One that knows when the end is; not even Jesus His Son knows until He gets the word. It could be at any moment, but that decision belongs to Him alone. Only the Father knows because He's the One that knows the final order of all things. He holds all things together in His hands including the earth on its axis, the gravitational pull, the planets, and all the stars and how they align. Thank you, Father, Son, and precious Holy Spirit.

Chapter 13
Going Deeper in Your Destiny

> "Deep calls unto deep at the noise of Your waterfalls; All Your waves and billows have gone over me. The LORD will command His loving-kindness in the daytime, and in the night His song shall be with me…." (Psalm 42:7, 8)

God wants us to go into the deep places with Him. I don't know about you, but I'm tired of this surface level stuff, I want the deeper things of God. I want to be able to tap into the mysteries of God. I don't just want to see His mighty acts but I want to better understand and know His ways. As a minor digs down deep into the crust of the earth to mine for the treasures of the earth I want to go deeper in the things of God and hit the main vein of heaven. I want to hit the vein where the gold is hidden.

Friends, there is a main vein in the realm of the Spirit and it is there for all of us to find it. Those who have tapped into it before won't settle for anything less. The deep things of God are what we should be seeking after especially as it pertains to our true purpose and destiny. The same is true for the sperm of a man. It has to travel very far inside the reproductive parts of a woman and has to go through many obstacles in order to fertilize her eggs, but again, only one out of thousands has to get there for destiny to be birthed.

For me, and my destiny experience, I was impregnated early. The divine Seed of heaven (Jesus Christ) got down deep on the inside of my heart and I was quickly impregnated with my very reason for being. It was the seed called vision. Since my early teens I have been in labor with the call of God upon my life. I was blessed that the Lord chose to use me early in my relationship with Him. Almost from the very first moment I received Jesus Christ He began using me and brought me before the people of God to minister. I've been on a long journey in this thing called purpose and destiny. I was one who as they say "got pregnant early in life." How many ladies reading this book can say in the natural "hey, that was me, I got pregnant early in life?" Some of you really know and can relate to what I'm talking about. Some ladies get pregnant very early in life and others farther down the road.

Yes men, I am a man, I know it's hard to swallow but I got pregnant, and I was only sixteen. Now ladies, because I am a man, you may be asking yourself again "how in the world can this guy identify with me?" Well, in Christ, it can happen and it will continue to happen every single day, yes, even to men! Since the beginning of time there have been so many great men and women of God throughout the generations of time who have gone before us that have experienced this same spiritual pregnancy. There will continue to be countless more, both men and women, who will continue to experience the very same thing after we are gone, but I want to be counted among that number and I want you to be counted too.

Pregnancy is not a sprint, it is a long distance run just as getting to your purpose and destiny is not a sprint. The question is, are you ready to go the distance? further, are you ready to go deep with God? One of the very first things I tell all of my ministry training candidates at Gateway

International Bible Institute is that ministry is a long distance run. That no matter how hard they try to look for a shortcut, there are none.

History is filled with men and women who literally gave their very lives for the purpose that God had called them to. Did you know that? Did you know the Word of God is precious? Many great men and women of God have spilt their blood and gave their very lives for the book we call the Holy Bible. They gave birth to their destiny, and in doing so, some gave birth to martyrdom. As tragic as it is, just like in natural childbirth some women give their very lives just to give birth to their babies, so too these men and woman gave their very lives pushing out their destinies so we could have the Bible. I don't believe that many Americans can appreciate that anymore or really know what that means, but people in other countries know what giving birth to their destiny means. Sometimes it could mean giving their very lives for the sake of the Gospel of Jesus Christ. That is what a true life's purpose and destiny is. It's being faced with the possibility of dying for your purpose and then being willing to give up your very life - willingly to fulfill your ultimate destiny.

> Then Peter began to say to Him, "See, we have left all and followed You." So Jesus answered and said, "Assuredly, I say to you, there is no one who has left house or brothers or sisters or father or mother or wife or children or lands, for My sake and the gospel's, who shall not receive a hundredfold now in this time." (Mark 10:28-30)

Some of you are shocked at these words right now, I know. Remember, we are talking about giving birth to our life's TRUE purpose and destiny! That's why it's so important to know what our purpose and destiny is. Some of you reading this book are already in many figurative ways giving your life (and in some cases figuratively of course - giving your blood) for things that have absolutely nothing to do with your calling and destiny.

For example, many professional men and women give all they possibly can to their companies and for the corporations that have employed them. As these professionals have, or will, find out, no number, no mark, no quota or goal ever seems to be good enough. In fact, when you meet or exceed these company goals they will then begin to expect them all the time from you and its' almost like they are asking for your life's blood!

But remember just as how a woman becomes pregnant and has to begin to recognize that her life is no longer her own and can't live for herself any longer but now has to live sacrificially for the sake of another growing on the inside of her tummy. To really live out your life's true purpose and destiny you can no longer live for yourself or your company or whatever else is sucking the lifeblood out of you. You must now begin to live every day for that new life that God placed there on the inside of you. Your destiny is growing and developing on the inside of your spiritual womb.

We have a motto that we all try to live by at Desert Rose Community Church which is that God is first, family is second, church and ministry third, vocation is fourth and everything else falls in line from there on. When the time comes for us to make choices for our future, we all need to make the right ones.

In Hebrews 12:2-3 it says, "Looking unto Jesus, the author and the finisher of our faith, who for the joy that was set before Him endured the cross...." Jesus was faithful to His purpose and His destiny, and the verse continues; "and has sat down at the right hand of the throne of God." "For consider Him who endured such hostility from sinners against Himself, lest you become weary and discouraged in your souls." Jesus has already suffered and gave His very life and blood for you so you no longer have to, so stop doing it because others put the demand upon you to! He gave His blood sacrificially so that we don't ever have to. Tell your soul to praise the Lord and to come alive in your purpose and destiny. Tell yourself you are blessed! You don't live your life for all the bloodsuckers around you. You live your life for God and in and through Him you can fulfill your life's true purpose and destiny! Do not allow yourself to grow weary in well doing in your search. Press hard after God, and you will give birth.

> "And let us not grow weary while doing good, for in due season we shall reap if we do not lose heart." (Galatians 6:9)

Your Appointed Time to Give Birth

When destiny begins to push it's way out of a believers life it is like a baby growing on the inside of a woman's womb until that exact moment in time comes for the baby to be born to fulfill its ultimate plan and purpose. The same is true as purpose develops and grows inside of a believer. We are impregnated with the Seed of heaven in the spiritual womb of our lives. However, just as in pregnancy in the natural, that which we have been impregnated with in the spirit is not made a reality until God says it is your "Chronos," time. In other words, your appointed moment in time, for the purposes of God to be manifest through you. That is what Chronos means, the appointed moment in time for the purposes of God to be birthed in the earth. Chronos is the Greek word where we get our word "chronological" from. Some of you were born at 7:00a.m., some at 3:00 a.m. Whatever time it may have been, it was a Chronos moment, the appointed moment in time for the purposes of God to begin in your life. It was the exact moment in time for your mother to give birth to your destiny. The same is true with our purpose and destiny in Christ. When it's 'Chronos time' it is the exact moment, the appointed moment in time for vision to be birthed in us by the power of the Holy Spirit that begins to manifest in the natural realm we live in. It is when we begin to manifest our purpose in the earth, and to fulfill the days that were pre-fashioned for us by God, that our ultimate God-ordained purpose and destiny in the physical realm begins to come forth.

> "Your eyes saw my substance, being yet unformed. And in Your book they all were written, the days fashioned for me, when as yet there were none of them." (Psalm 139:16)

When purpose and destiny begin to become manifested in our Chronos time the Bible says the very earth begins to groan in travail.

> "For the earnest expectation of the creation eagerly waits for the revealing of the sons of God." (Romans 8:19)

> "For we know that the whole creation groans and labors with birth pangs together until now, Not only that, but we also who have the first fruits of the Spirit, even we ourselves groan within ourselves...." (Romans 8:21-23)

These wonderful passages lead us to believe that even the whole earth is in travail, giving birth, waiting and expecting for our true purpose and destinies to be born and manifested. Think about this, before we were even born, the whole earth groaned and travailed for moms to give birth because it's those human beings, us, who become the manifest sons of God. In a Chronos moment, you and I were born and became the manifested sons and daughters of God in the earth. Every moment, hour, and every day the earth groans and cries out as in travail for the manifested sons of God to be born, just as a woman moans and travails in childbearing.

A few thousand years ago, the earth gave birth to her first-born son Adam in the Garden of Eden. Then it was heavens turn! Heaven gave birth to the second Adam and God pushed Him - Jesus Christ the One and only begotten Son of the Father into the earth over two thousand years ago, Hallelujah! Now there are more sons, daughters, and children of God being born, the earth is groaning for more because now through Jesus Christ we have become the true manifested sons of God in the earth. We continue to reveal heavens plans and purposes for the earth through our lives in God's Son Jesus Christ. Are you ready to continue to push to keep the process going? Remember you are a son, or daughter of God. You are now another manifested son of God on the earth and destined for greatness! It's not just time – it's your Chronos time! Your set time for your divine destiny to be manifested in the earth!

Chapter 14
No Pain, No Gain

Ladies, not to diminish your hardship in any way, but again I think the closest I have ever come, as a man, to experience the agony of childbirth is when I had kidney stones. How many of you men have ever had kidney stones before? I've never felt such excruciating pain in all my life. I thought I was going to die and when the doctor showed me the stones on the x-ray, I was shocked! The Doctor came into the room in the ER in which I was placed. I was loopy by that time because of a large shot of morphine (what I am calling the equivalent to an epidural for men). The doctor was trying to show me what was causing me such horrible pain. He said, "Mr. Alton, you see the microscopic objects going down this area here that kind of resembles a strand of hair? You have three of those microscopic objects there trying to pass through."

I looked at my wife with great disbelief and a kind of a silly "I'm really not being a wimp here" expression and said, "No way, you said a kidney stone, not a microscopic object! You need to re-take these x-rays! That little dinky microscopic thing is what's causing me such pain?!" When I first heard it was kidney stones, I didn't think of something as small as a grain of sand. Man I pictured a stone, or a boulder something man-sized! Ohhhh, it hurt so badly! I'm telling you ladies, I gave birth to those things and it was triplets. Needless to say that ladies told me that what I felt was only remotely minor compared to what you women feel when you give birth to your babies. The pain I felt was indescribable. I can't even comprehend what it must feel like to birth a child through such a small, narrow birthing canal. Women, how do you do that?

I may fall short as a man in this way, but in the spiritual realm of my life, I've had to carry the spiritual fetus of divine purpose for a long time. As some women find themselves in labor for many hours in the hospital room pushing out the dream and vision of having a baby, I too, have experienced many years of long and intense labor pains in the spiritual womb of my life. Men, this is how we, too, can give birth to things. As I stated before in the natural I am the father of three wonderful children: my Abbi Rose, and my two boys, Michael, and, Brian James. They are all miracle children and each one has their own miraculous story. It's because of my first born son Brian James (we endearingly call him B.J. for short) that I believe I know so much first hand information about giving birth because of the incredible events that surrounded his birth. What I now call his day of destiny. I believe God allowed these things to happen in my life and his life in order to teach me and help me to understand some things for the day that I would write this book on destiny. He wanted me to understand about all the intricacies of birth and how things are suppose to flow, function, and work out in the process as well as how some things can go wrong.

My first wife of 10 years Alyce, B.J's birthmother, is no longer living, she passed away due to major illness. Our first child was conceived and was born very premature and didn't live more than a few hours.

Trying to make a very long and traumatic story as short as possible, Alyce had trouble holding children inside of her womb. Essentially the cervix in a woman's body is what holds everything in until it's delivery time, and though we were not aware of it for a long time, medically she had what is called a weak cervix. That is why our first child was premature, and because of that fact, the baby came too early so therefore she had to give birth to that child as if she was full term. She pushed just a few short times and the baby came out very tiny and severely undeveloped. When he came out he didn't cry and only lived for a few minutes and as my father looked on and my mother Racheal had her arms around me, I held that little baby in my hands until he died in my arms and returned back to heaven peacefully.

It was one of the most difficult and challenging moments in my life up to that point and even more so for Alyce. It was absolutely heart breaking as we both had such high expectations that God had children in mind for our lives and I personally was really holding onto that. You see I truly believed that God had promised me a fist born son. You know, when God promises you something and you see it born and all of a sudden it dies in your hands right before your very eyes, that is a difficult place to be.

Have you ever been there before? I held that baby in my hands and I watched that little life die. He was so small, really small. He was just cupped in the palm of my hand. It was really hard because this tiny baby embodies God's promise to me. It took a long time but I was finally able to get through that and turn it over fully to the Lord. Deep in my heart I still held onto the promise that He gave me before all this had happened and somehow the Holy Spirit helped me to heal and I didn't allow myself to become bitter at God over it. I still believed that God was good, and even though this happened, He would still find a way to keep His promise. I didn't give up because somehow deep on the inside I knew that having a son would be a part of my life's true purpose and destiny. God had always been faithful to His promises in the past and I believed that somehow, someway, that promise would be fulfilled in my life.

You know, up to this point in my life I had very much likened myself and my life to someone in the Bible. Maybe you have someone in the Bible you identify with, too. Maybe you identify with Esther, or Ruth, or Sarah, or for the men you may identify with Joseph, Samuel, Isaiah or perhaps Jeremiah. Throughout my life, I have identified with King David. Have you ever had a time when you were backslidden (far away from God) and had gotten away from your purpose and destiny? This is where I was in my life; I was trying to figure it all out for God and I was telling Him how things were going to go in my life, and I was doing it my way. My first wife and I got pregnant out of wedlock. There were many other things that were centered on that sin, so I could totally identify with the story of David and Bathsheba.

Do you remember that whole tragic story? David moaned and he wept when his son died because of his sin of adultery with her and the hit he put on her husband Uriah so that he could have things his way. After Bathsheba gave birth to the child, it died almost instantly. As all this was happening, David fasted and wept until he got up and cleaned himself off and then moved forward in his calling, purpose, and destiny.

Although some of the details of the story are different in like manner, that's pretty much what happened to me. I was in the very place with God in my circumstance (see II Samuel 11). Then our second baby, Brian James (BJ), came along. During his conception is when we discovered the reason for our last loss. New testing from expert OB/GYN doctors revealed that Alyce had a weak cervix. That means she couldn't really hold the baby in the womb as woman are made to do.

Thank God for specialists who had practical ideas about how we could actually have a baby in spite of this difficult diagnosis. Our specialist was one of the best in the country when it came to treating and working with this kind of diagnosis. Let me tell you right now that when

God has a plan for your life He will divinely connect you with the right people that can make His will happen on earth for your destiny to be complete. Anyway, this particular doctor was only here in Arizona for a few months, but he decided to take our case on as a 'special project.'

I knew it was a God initiated miracle at the time, but with that said, you know how some doctors can be. Unfortunately, many doctors have a God complex and think they are God in the flesh. I knew that even if the doctor didn't know it that God orchestrated that special decision. He studied Alyce's case very intently and suggested that we allow him to perform a cutting edge procedure called a "cerclage."

To perform a cerclage a surgeon would add string type stitches to close the cervix shut. This surgery is intended to enable a woman to carry a baby to at least the third trimester. Sometimes the surgery lasts a long time and sometimes it's just barely long enough for premature babies to have a good chance at life. After many intensely difficult discussions, we decided it was worth the risk because God had made a promise and we were taking Him at His Word. We took the risk and Alyce had the procedure. It was a cutting edge surgery at the time and it went wonderfully. This type of surgery enabled her to carry BJ almost a whole month longer than she had carried the first baby we had previously lost, but the drawback was that she literally had to stay in bed the whole time with her feet elevated, the entire length of the pregnancy. Ladies maybe some of you have had complicated pregnancies too and can relate to this. Boy was that a hard time in both of our lives. You can only imagine what kind of pressure that put on our marriage. I was young, stupid, selfish, and behaving like an immature man at that time. We married young so we were both still growing up into adulthood and didn't really anticipate so many difficulties so soon. I had to grow up quickly as a man in this marriage and I was dealing with some selfish feelings and some other issues that I was working through at this time of my life. Men, all I can say is that we sure can be some pretty big babies in a grown up body sometimes. I'm sure that all of you ladies reading this book right now are saying to yourself, "You GO Pastor Brian. Come on and tell it... Amen!"

Because of the severity of the situation, my parents had to help us both on many occasions during this time. As she got farther along in her pregnancy, we had to move out of the little two-bedroom apartment we were living in a rundown part of Glendale, Arizona. We had to ask my parents if we could move into their home to help monitor and take care of Alyce's daily physical and medical needs as well as help us out financially. Although I had decent insurance coverage at that time while working for the city of Peoria, our medical bills were mounting up so much that we couldn't keep up with them. I was so thankful that they took us in as I knew that I couldn't work a full time job, take care of all her needs, worry about the other medical things too, and all of the 'what ifs.'

Maybe you can relate to what I'm talking about 'what if this happens?' or 'what if that happens?' Thank God for good caring loving parents. I don't know what I would have done without all of their love, help, and support. I will always be indebted to them for this. Thank you so much for being there Mom and Dad. Although things were very difficult and trialing at times for both Alyce and myself (mainly for poor Alyce who was stuck confined in my parents house for months in our bed laying with her feet up in the air) things seemed to be holding up well medically with the pregnancy for several months.

The cerclage seemed to be holding things within the uterus as the OB/GYN had expected it to, but about six and a half months into her pregnancy things began to go desperately wrong. Although this extremely intense summer Saturday happened 21 years ago, I remember it like it was yesterday. We were having a really good weekend, Alyce was feeling good enough to come downstairs to watch some television on the couch, we had a nice lunch, watched some movies, we were laughing at silly things, and we were just starting to talk about what we were going to have for dinner that night. It was a peaceful easy day with no real excitement. I remember thinking to myself that this was one of the most restful and peaceful days that I personally have had in a very long time. Then all of a sudden, out of nowhere, the weekend took a turn for the worst like something terrible out of a bad nightmare or something.

Doing nothing but what doctors told her to do, there were no sudden movements, pulling or stretching motions, falls, or accidents to cause what would come as a huge shock to all of us. All of a sudden, Alyce felt as if the cerclage stitches had torn and she felt water go running down her leg. I don't mean to be graphic, but you can just imagine what she and I were going through. She cried out, "Brian, I can't believe it's happening to me again! What are we going to do?" I ran over to her and began to pray over her and comfort her. I had heard that panicked voice with light fluttered cry of paranoia before so I started praying aloud. "Lord, Jesus NO! No, I refuse to believe that you allowed her to carry the baby this long and feel him growing inside her womb, and will allow us to lose another baby!" There she was crying, mascara dripping down her face and with water running down her legs. I could see it running down the inside of her thighs and falling down and soaking into the floor. A spirit of dread and fear tried sweeping over my very soul as I watched that scene. It was as almost as if I could hear the devil saying to me "It's happening again... Where is your God now?" I remember telling my parents and they were just as shocked and horrified as I was. My mom began to cry and pray over us. I quickly packed a few things and ran and retrieved the OB/GYN's phone number and began to dial it as I loaded her into the car in order to rush her to the nearest emergency room.

Can you imagine the terror and the panic that rushed through us? As I was driving the car, right at that moment, I began to tell the devil that he was a liar and I said out loud, "But God, you promised!" I was in sheer panic and horror the whole way. This scene had become all too familiar to us after many doctor's visits throughout the pregnancy. She calmed herself down and I acted as everything was going to be fine, we arrived and went hobbling into the emergency room. Our doctor had everything ready and prepared for her so when we walked in the door and told them her name they immediately rushed her back to a delivery surgical room.

The Lord had laid it on my heart to go pray so I said, "I'm so sorry but I can't follow you in right now, I have to go and pray." I felt so bad, you know, I was torn, my wife and my baby. I knew in my spirit I had to go and pray and get a hold of the Father to contend for this baby's destiny. It was perfect timing because just as I said those words a wonderful caring nurse she recognized and trusted from our last visit ran up to her side and said "don't worry I am here to help you." She went up to the third floor with her and I went in to the hospital Chapel and I knelt down on the prayer kneeler at that little altar and there I began to remind the Lord of His promise, "Lord, You said... You said that I would have a son!" Almost immediately, it was as if the enemy came in and said, "God lied to you, He let you down again. You have served Him, and this is the reward you get?"

Friends, you need to know that it's those toughest and longest dark moments of our lives that the enemy will try to breathe his fowl lies into your ears to get you to believe there is no hope. He will come to wear you down at the most vulnerable moments in life because he knows it's when we are at our weakest. In situations like what I am describing, you can either believe what God said, or you can believe the lies of the enemy. Each will have their own outcome and fulfillment in a person's destiny. One leads to life, liberty and freedom, and the other to bitterness, defeat, and ultimately death. All the outward circumstances seemed to dictate defeat and death, but God's word to me was, "You will have a son." I said, "Devil, you are a liar, you are the chief of liars."

I began to pray in the Spirit for that life to come into the world. I felt like Abraham, remember when father Abraham took his son Isaac up to the top of mount Moriah. On top of that mountain Abraham had everything but the ram he needed for the sacrifice. He went up on top of that mountain in Israel and he had to bind his own son on the altar. Remember, this was the promised son that God had given to him, but now it was looking as if he was going to have to sacrifice him to fulfill God's purpose and destiny for their lives. As disappointing and as difficult as that was for him to become completely obedient to God's purposes, Abraham pulled the sharp sacrificial knife out of its sheath, lifted it high to the sky, and began to bring it forth to do God's will. He was stopped from sacrificing his son just in the nick of time only to be shown that God had already provided a ram for the sacrifice (see Genesis 22).

Like Abraham of old I went into that Chapel and I said with tears streaming down my face, "Lord, as difficult as it is for me I give this child back to You if Your ultimate purpose requires me to let him go, I will do it; He is yours." Do you know what it took for me to do that? It took everything inside of me. At that moment, as incredibly difficult as it was, I had to die to the promise, because fulfilling God's ultimate plan and purpose for my life was greater. I could relate, although very minutely, to what Jesus prayed in the Garden of Gethsemane in Luke 22:42, "...nevertheless not my will, but thine be done." (KJV) You see, my garden was that hospital Chapel. "Lord," I prayed, "if You want him, take him, he's Yours. Not my will, but Your will be done."

Taking you back to the very moment Brian was actually born, I made it back into the delivery room as she began the process of delivering early. They began to work on Alyce and my son Brian and they had them both surrounded by two teams of medical personnel. I asked how it was going, and of course, when crazy things like that are going on in the delivery room, they didn't take the time to stop and tell me what was going on. All I could do was pray. Thank God I had received the gift of the Holy Spirit with the evidence of speaking with other tongues. I don't know what kind of prayer I could have prayed with my own understanding at that moment. I know God is a big God and He would have heard the cry of my heart no matter what I prayed, but I was able to pray intently, fervently, and authoritatively in that moment in tongues. I could feel faith arise in my soul and I began to say aloud in the delivery room in front of everyone, "Father God, I pray that you would breathe the breath of life – Your life into my son, Lord." That word just kept coming to me as I prayed in the spirit in tongues. I would continue to pray in the spirit, I would hear the word 'Zoë', and so I would pray, "Yes Lord, the Zoë breath of life! Just breathe upon my son Lord!" I started using that word repeatedly. It is very important to listen to what the Holy Spirit is saying when it comes to your purpose and destiny. I was praying that loudly; I'm telling you all the medical staff assisting us must have thought I was crazy. I was saying, "Devil, you can't come at us with fear and intimidation, I'm going to release faith and praise in this hospital room right now and my son is going to live and not die! He will breathe supernaturally in the name of Jesus!" I believe it was because of that I was able penetrate the heavens and see the breakthrough come! I cried out, "Lord Jesus, breathe the Zoë breath of life into my son" and all of a sudden I heard, "Wahhh!" It was not a big sound, but just the faintest, sweetest "wahhh" because he was so tiny. He was premature and very, small. Immediately, when I heard the soft sound of his voice, I knew that God had answered my prayer and fulfilled His promise to me. As difficult and as scary as it was, Alyce gave birth to my son Brian James that evening. He was three and a half months premature and only weighed 2 1/2 lbs. I was able to hold him in the palm of my hand. His precious little body only reached from the tip of my fingers to the end of the palm of my hand. Let me tell you, it was a battle of life and death over his destiny all the way. Alyce also almost lost her own life giving birth to him. She lost a lot of blood in the process of delivery. When she was done, they rushed her in one direction of the hospital to work on her and took Brian in another direction to work on him. I was standing there in the middle not quite knowing where to go or what to do. All I could do was keep calling on Jesus. I was told by medical staff that night that I could run the risk of losing one of them before the night was over, but I knew that I got it right with the Lord in that Chapel, whatever the future held in store for me. This all took place on Flag Day, June 14th 1988. The medical field had started to develop new technology for premature births back then, but there is so much more incredible medical technology in this area today. The Dr's were telling us back then that if this pregnancy was to be a success and the baby should live that it would have to be an absolute creative miracle. I knew that, along with all our divine intervention, Alyce and my new baby, Brian James, were going to get the best medical care possible.

I'm telling you God is the giver of life. He is the Author and the Finisher. God gives life, and He takes it away. He gives us breath and removes it. We all have an allotted time here on earth. When I heard that little, bitty voice coming from my son, my heart swelled with joy because God fulfilled His promise. I got to hold my baby this time and he didn't die, he lived and had the breath of heaven flowing through his premature lungs! I held him in my hand and he lived! It was the same scenario all over again that I had experienced with the first son we had lost. He had a bonnet on his head, and I held him in the palm of my hand. He was barely two pounds and he was looking at me. My promise was birthed and lived because God had a purpose and a destiny for me and now for Brian James. He gave me the ability to push; he was born and God breathed divine purpose and destiny into my son. At the time, I had just produced a worship tape; I felt led to put that tape in the incubator they placed him in, to fill his new life with thanksgiving and the praises of God. The nurses were so good to us. They would let it play continuously in his bed. When the batteries began to get low, they would get more and replace them so I wouldn't have to worry about the worship stopping. A couple of nurses testified in their own way that they could feel a special presence and the favor of God being released over my son as that worship music played. When the tape was playing on the floor, their unit was peaceful and all the other babies no matter how critical or minor their cases were they would somehow respond to the worship. Brian improved quickly and he began to eat. Within just a few short months he was able to come home on life support monitors. If we hadn't gone through the pain of this circumstance, we wouldn't have gained the experience of a divine miracle! I don't know what you've believed for, but I know that He's a God who answers prayer. I know that He is God and when He says something, He intends to do it. The doctors told us that my son would not breathe right, walk, talk, see, or hear right. They said his growth would be stunted. They said he would probably have a learning disability and would be developmentally delayed. I tell you, when God does something, He does it right. BJ is taller, better looking, and smarter than I am. He made good grades in school and was at the top of his class a few times, and he is multitalented in every way. In fact, he is one of the most talented kids we have in our church, and I'm not just bragging about him because he's my son; it's the truth. He's a precious young man and a natural born leader. He was a leader in the church youth group for years, and he plays the drums on our church worship team. What I am really trying to say in this testimony is that God's plan, purpose, and destiny for both my son and me defied all of the negative reports that the world, the flesh, and the devil gave to me and tried to put on Brian James. Without the pain of this difficult experience in my life, there could be no true understanding of my son Brian's birth and my promised destiny, nor could I truly and uniquely understand the purpose and role that Alyce and I played as his parents in his own purpose and destiny. As the saying goes, "No pain, No gain." Wherever you are in your own walk, be assured that what God has promised you as it relates to your purpose and destiny in Him, that He intends to deliver it and bring it to pass! Amen.

Chapter 15
Pregnant With Destiny

As I have stated in general before I now prophetically and directly declare to you by the unction of the Spirit of God again, that some of you are on the verge of giving birth. There are many of you no matter where you find yourself in life or what vocation you find yourself working in at this present time, you are called to preach the gospel of Jesus Christ. There is more in store for you, and there is more to your life than what you are doing in the everyday humdrum. You will become ordained men and women (preachers) of the Gospel of Jesus Christ. For some of you your pulpit will be in church buildings, others will be in office buildings or retail stores, local schools and college campuses, some in government buildings, and still others may not be in a building at all but on the highways and byways of mission fields around the world. Wherever that place is, you will begin to manifest your destiny in Jesus Christ. By the way, as a little side note, preaching is not at all exclusive only to men, but women can preach the Gospel as well! Let me go out on a limb and say that women are called into the ministry just as much as men are. Now I hope I didn't just lose some readers because of their particular viewpoints, backgrounds, and church traditions over this truthful statement. I Praise God for the many faithful servant hearted women that have surrounded my wife Phaedra and I in our ministry. I don't know where we would be without them. There was a time when the number of women out numbered the amount of men in our fellowship, but thanks be to God, the ratio of men has balanced out the overwhelming number of faithful women. I think this is true of most American churches today. Dear ladies, please don't let anyone, denomination or corporation limit you or discriminate you because of your gender. God used just as many women as He did men to accomplish His Kingdom purposes in the earth.

Let me say that just as a pregnant woman gives off a certain shimmering glow, I see prophetically that some of you are bursting with the glow of excitement as your spiritual pregnancy of purpose and destiny develops. Yet there are still others who have lost their divine glow because they have miscarried a few times as it relates to their destiny. Like my story, you tried to give birth and the baby died before your eyes and now you can't take the pain of birthing again, but I tell you that you can become pregnant again! You can give birth to your purpose, to your dream, and to your destiny because it's God's will! Habakkuk 2:14 says, "For the earth will be filled with the knowledge of the glory of the Lord, as the waters cover the sea."

Now that is a very bold prophetic declaration. How do you suppose that is going to happen? How is the Lord going to fill the earth with the knowledge of His glory like the waters cover the sea? The answer is that He is doing it through you and me! Remember that we are the manifested sons and daughters of God, being birthed in the earth to fulfill His purpose and destiny from the foundations of the world. Even with all the generations that have gone before us, the knowledge of the glory of the Lord has not filled the entire world yet. So therefore, YOU can become pregnant again! If you are pregnant now, rejoice, because there is a purpose for you to give birth to your very own destiny that is wrapped up in God's ultimate plan and purpose to reveal the knowledge of His glory to the earth through YOU! Maybe you've had some lost dreams, or the circumstances of your life have killed your baby (your vision) off, but you can still be fruitful in the spiritual womb of your life.

God wants to re-impregnate you right here and right now. He wants to implant 'His dream' for you inside the spiritual womb of your life. Let Him love you, move in and through you, and 'know' you. Remember, the Bible speaks about a man 'knowing' a woman and almost all the time it translates into intimacy and relationship. Love Him; He loves you, and He desires you. Like the wonderful passionate love story in the book of Song of Solomon the "Beloved" (type and shadow of Jesus) desired the "Shulamite" woman (type and shadow of us and the Church), let the Lord impregnate you with His Spirit. Let Him overshadow you and impregnate you with something heavenly and divine as He did with Mary the mother of Jesus. I am foreseeing (divinely seeing potential, events purposed in God before they happen or could possibly happen) things as it pertains to the destinies of those reading this book. Satan's chief mission is to try to stop the truth of this message from truly affecting you, penetrating you, and impregnating you. He (the devil) desires to get you off your path. We are a threat to him and to the kingdom of darkness. Don't allow the enemy to have his way. See things through until you're fully living out your divine purpose and destiny. Stand guard over the seeds of truth being released into the spiritual womb of your life and be in prayer. As the umbilical cord feeds the baby inside a womb, feed upon God with the Word, worship, and prayer. Seek after more of God's plan, purpose, and will for your life.

Breathing Through the Contractions

Men, we have to learn, just as the women do in natural birth, how to breathe through our spiritual contractions. Sometimes life's difficulties and problems will bring contractions into our life (extreme pressure upon us). Pregnant women, however, are taught to do something extremely vital during the pressure of their contractions however light or intense. That's right, they are taught to "breathe." Spiritually we have to learn how to breathe through intense moments of our lives while we are pregnant with God's plan, purpose, and dreams, that is living on the inside of the spiritual womb of our lives. How we learn to "breathe" is through the coaching of the Holy Spirit when we come into the presence of God. In fact, just take a deep breath in the Spirit right now. Whatever contractions you have been breathing through today, however light or intense don't lose your direction just breathe... As the old worship song says, "Turn your eyes upon Jesus. Look full in His wonderful face and the things of earth will grow strangely dim in the light of His glory and grace." You need to begin to seek the Lord daily through worship and prayer. This helps prepare you for whatever stretching, developing, or intense pressure that may come your way as you press toward your life's purpose and destiny. Songs like, "Come Holy Spirit, I need thee, come sweet Spirit I pray, come in your strength and your power, come in your own gentle way."

Jesus said in John 1:4 (paraphrased) that "He was life and His life is the light of men." His life, His seed, the divine Seed of heaven, has been breathed into your spiritual womb. It's not about you, it's about what you are carrying on the inside of you. It's about purpose, destiny, and a greater Master Plan than the one you're living now. God is trying to birth Kingdom things in you and establish His divine will on earth through you. So you have to learn how to breathe through the contractions of your life, and you don't breathe while watching television, while eating, or through another relationship, and you don't breathe through other substances that would numb your mind, will and emotions. You breathe in the "Zoë breath" of life in God.

I just love the worship song "You are the air I breathe" as I feel that it depicts through its lyrics and primarily its chorus the greatest example of breathing in the Holy Spirit. It is a song that draws the manifested presence of God and allows us to "breathe" spiritually through the contractions of our lives. Why do we sing songs like this and others like it? Is it just for the lyrical beauty, feel good melody of the chorus, or the crescendo of the bridge that leads us to an emotional high? Why do believers sing worship songs like this? It's to be able to "breathe" in the creative life of the Lord! It's to help us gain new life and stamina through all the difficult contractions of life so that we can continue to push out our divine purpose and destiny, and so that He can continue to breathe creative life into us.

This is why worship songs are birthed out of the heavenly realm. They breakthrough the heavenly dimension and break forth into the early dimension and become creatively planted inside the spiritual womb of psalmists with songs like "You are the air I breathe." God is trying to get us to hear and know the sound of heaven. There is a sound that goes beyond the natural ear and reaches the spiritual ear. That's why in Revelation 2:7 it says, "He who has an ear, let him hear what the Spirit says to the churches." There is a sound that can impregnate you in the spiritual womb of your life. It can help others to breathe through their contractions in order to birth forth their purpose and destinies, not just for the encouragement and blessing of the Church, but worship songs that can change a city, transform a nation, and reach the world.

We are called to release the Kingdom of God on earth as it is in heaven. Again, how we breathe in spiritually is through praise, worship and prayer. The Spirit of God is trying help you understand that you have got to breathe through your spiritual pregnancy, your purpose, discovering who you are, what you are made for and why you're here on earth! Being able to breathe through some of the most extreme spiritual contractions of your life is vital to be able to fully recognize your true purpose and destiny. Often times a person will realize their destiny in some of the most extreme conditions and situations. This is the very reason why a single mother's faith and courage to breathe and push through her own life's painful contractions led to a man's capture by police by the name of Brian Nichols in Atlanta, Georgia:

On Monday, March 14th, 2005 on the front page of the Atlanta Journal-Constitution there was a photograph of a very special woman by the name of Ashley Smith. Ignoring political correctness, the headline proclaimed, "An Angel Sent From God." All of Atlanta said, "Amen."

In the end, a man by the name Brian Nichols surrendered peacefully, but not before he terrorized the Metro Atlanta area with a killing spree that started in a Fulton County Courthouse and touched off the largest manhunt in Georgia history. He was able to evade capture for 26 hours, beating down or shooting anyone who got in his way, until, that is, he crossed paths with a brave young single mom with a purpose and destiny.

Ashley Smith, was the 26 year old hostage who notified police that the Atlanta Courthouse Killer wanted to turn himself in, but not before she read to him from "The Purpose Driven Life" (written by Pastor Rick Warren), then shared her personal faith, read him the Bible and prayed for more than seven hours in her one-bedroom, Duluth, Georgia apartment. Nichols eventually told Ashley Smith that he believed she was an angel that God sent to him to show him the pain that he had caused others.

As she began to "breathe" through that very difficult situation in her own purpose and destiny by reading to him, sharing her faith, praying and worshipping through, it caused Nichols to change. As Ashley breathed in the Spirit of God, it helped her to push through the pain of that intense scene and released the Spirit of God to work in her and through her. Because of that, Brian Nichols came under dourest of the anointing of Smith's divine purpose and destiny that blocked out the demonic realm and the dark forces, those destructive lying spirits, and silenced the chemical imbalance and voices of mental illness. All of a sudden he started thinking about what everyone in the world thinks about from generation to generation, "Why am I here? Why was I born? What am I doing here? Why did I do this or that in my life? Where am I going from here, where will I spend eternity?"

We've been doing a lot of talking about purpose, but the subject truly comes to life when we can see purpose and destiny in the headlines. So, what is your purpose and destiny? God is speaking to you, and he is speaking to the Church! I am trying to impregnate you with this word like Ashley Smith with Brian Nichols so that maybe you can go and help other people understand what the Spirit of God is saying to them and to the Church in this hour about their divine purpose and destiny.

If you are not in a church that is not speaking, worshipping, and praying forth the fresh sound of heaven, then run from that church as fast as you can! As an apostolic and prophetic minister to this generation, I declare to you, find a church that is not only tuned in to heaven and hearing, but has the courage to speak forth what they are hearing! You need to find a Bible believing church where the Senior Pastor and the pastoral team are teaching and promoting the discovery of people's purpose, destiny, and spiritual gifts, as well as leaders who display confidence in who they are in their own destiny and calling and will not be threatened by yours in any way. If you're currently in a ministry that appears to be deaf, stale, and lifeless, then it's time to get out of the old revelation and into the newness of life and refreshing stream of what the Lord is saying and doing "now" in the church. That church had its purpose at one time I'm sure, it more than likely helped to lay a good foundation in your life, and there were good layers of revelation, knowledge and understanding that helped you walk victoriously for a season. Isaiah 43:19 says it best in this case. "Behold, I will do a new thing, now it shall spring forth; shall you not know it? I will even make a road in the wilderness and rivers in the desert."

Maybe some of that "old-time religion" has become like a dry barren desert to you. You're parched, and you're thirsty, inside your spiritual womb. I'm telling you that God wants to bring refreshing to your life. He wants to deposit the sound of heaven, and He wants to bring down those special things that are in the heavenlies over you and your destiny. He wants you to grasp those things and pull them down into the earthly realm. God is very serious about these things, and He is serious about your spiritual life. He is serious about His intimacy and His relationship with each and every one of you. He's serious about your willingness to trust Him and He wants to help you become all you were designed and created to be.

The Lord deposited something powerful on the inside of your spiritual womb. He's the Father of that and He wants to see it manifest before His eyes, and He wants you to see it through until it's birthed and manifested in the earth. The Father has had a divine plan for you since the very beginning of your life. Psalm 22:9-10 says, "But You are He who took Me out of the womb; You made Me trust while on My mother's breasts. I was cast upon You from birth. From My mother's womb You have been My God." Some of you are bit older in natural age and you're saying, "When God, when?" And the Lord just keeps saying to you "Push, you're almost there...hold on just a couple more hours, a few more days, few short weeks, a couple more months, or a few more years." Whatever time span in the pushing process you're in don't despise your time of preparation! God knows exactly when your water is supposed to break. Then when it does it will gush forth, contractions will begin, but remember to keep breathing through them and push! God knows when it's time. The Bible says some things are a mystery, and they are not for us to understand. They're just a mystery. If you're feeling barren in the spiritual womb of your life just keep saying, "Lord, Jesus! Send your rain!" "Lord, impregnate me with You; with my purpose and destiny." I pray that enormous vision, passion, and purpose that is burning on the inside of you is going to become clearer so you can understand it better. My prayer is that the Lord is going to breathe upon you and help you discover your purpose.

God wants us to be able to foresee and then passionately pursue. That's why the Lord speaks from heaven and touches someone's heart like Pastor Tommy Tenney to start writing about chasing after and perusing the presence of God. "The God Chasers" books are all about people following Him because deep down in the spiritual wombs of our lives they desperately desire more of Him. Amen! We all want to know and see Him more! God wants us all to foresee it, He wants us to know it, He wants us to understand it, and He wants each and every one of us to passionately pursue our future. The Lord has a future for every person born on the face of the earth. The whole earth labors and groans together for the manifested sons of God. You have been born for a reason, you're not just here taking up space. You are pregnant with purpose and destiny and you will give birth. Just keep breathing through the contractions of life and you will eventually bring forth God's Kingdom manifested in your purpose and destiny.

Chapter 16
Don't Lose Your Passion

Purpose is what releases your God given destiny upon the earth. Passion is the motorized vehicle that will take you there. So if you want to get somewhere with your purpose you have to get passionate about it. You've got to live your purpose, and as we said in the last chapter, you've got to breathe it. You've got to sleep on it, wake up on it, pray on it, write about it, sing about it, talk about it, preach about it, and prophecy about it. If you feel as if your dream has died, don't worry, your time will come:

> "Sing, O barren, You who have not borne! Break forth into singing, and cry aloud, You who have not labored with child! For more are the children of the desolate Than the children of the married woman, says the LORD." (Isaiah 54:1)

According to the Word of God, there is hope in Christ for all those who have been barren. The promise to you is that you can give birth too! You're going to have a spiritual purpose and destiny, too! The promise is that you become double fertile and you are going to have a quiver that is full of God's best! So sing oh barren one! When we breathe, pray, or we worship it releases supernatural power.

I believe that praise is the power of heaven, and this helps break your negative, stinking thinking. When you're out there in the real world and you start looking like the dustman and not the spirit man, when you begin to praise, and breathe, the water comes. When you sing, "Come Holy Spirit, I need thee," you begin to be washed off, things begin to break off, and transform, your emotions settle, and your heart stops beating so fast. Your attitude starts turning back around, and this is key because this is where your passion starts to build again, and you become a lighter person. You're no longer the nasty, negative person that you were when you last walked in the front door to your home, your office, or your church.

Let's get real; It doesn't matter how good of a person you think you are, or how long you've been in the Lord, what title you bear, what ministry you have or future ministry you want to have, we all get dusty sometimes. When you worship something begins to shift inside your stinking thinking. Your thoughts start slowly becoming His thoughts, and His thoughts start becoming your thoughts. God's ways are higher than our ways; His thoughts are higher than our thoughts. So are the heavens above the earth, and His ways above our ways. The Lord wants to bring the heavenly realm into our lives and invade the earthly realm of our lives.

If His ways are higher than our ways, He has to cause those things that are in the heavenlies to come down to earth. He wants heaven and earth to touch; He wants to bring that heavenly realm, thought, plan and purpose into the natural realm. He wants to bring it out of time, space, and eternity. He wants to bring it down into the "Chronos" time that we live in. He wants to birth it into the earth and inside of us. He wants us to not only understand it, but also to become extremely passionate about it. This will happen when we yield the spiritual womb of our life to be impregnated with the divine Seed of heaven. So, when we worship we are opening up our womb to be impregnated and passionate with the things of heaven. When you yield yourself to Him in prayer and worship, you not only receive fresh revelation but you become passionate.

This is the kind of thing that helps you understand all the craziness you just went through with your boss or maybe that rude bill collector that got a hold of you. Maybe it was the flat tire on your way to work, the IRS, the misunderstanding with "sister so-and-so" at church. It might be relationship issues with your spouse, or that difficult situation with your children. You begin to have a new understanding and no matter what the situation you remain passionate about your purpose and destiny. The divine Seed of heaven comes down and bursts forth revelation, and your thoughts become illuminated and become His thoughts, your old ways now become His new way, and now because you have His thoughts and you have His ways you remain passionate no matter what comes your way and you are not moved by any other circumstance. You are only moved by the One who moves you, Jesus Christ! It's time to quit playing silly games with your life. When you can slow yourself down enough to hear your mind, your thoughts start to shift and you begin to come into agreement with the Spirit of God and with the things of heaven. Your passion builds stronger and stronger as you begin to come into agreement with the words of faith that transcends the natural things. Hebrews 11:1 says, "Now faith is the substance of things hoped for, the evidence of things not seen." It first takes a passion to want to please God, and once your faith begins to please God, you begin to see and hear things you haven't heard or seen before. This is what God told the prophet Jeremiah.

> "For I know the thoughts that I think toward you, says the LORD, thoughts of peace and not of evil, to give you a future and a hope. Then you will call upon Me and go and pray to

> Me, and I will listen to you. And you will seek Me and find Me, when you search for Me with all your heart." (Jeremiah 29:11-13)

Passion for the things of God helps us to come into agreement with the heavenly realm; the realm that is over us with good things waiting to be released upon us.

> But as it is written: "Eye has not seen, nor ear heard, Nor have entered into the heart of man The things which God has prepared for those who love Him." But God has revealed them to us through His Spirit. For the Spirit searches all things, yes, the deep things of God." (I Corinthians 2:9, 10)

What is over us takes precedence over every natural order on this earth. God has prepared special blessings for all of us. While teaching the people about these kinds of blessings of the Kingdom, Jesus ran into a centurion who had extreme passion for his servant's well being, according to scripture it was obviously someone very near and dear to his heart, amazed by such faith and passion Jesus responds immediately with a heartfelt commendation of his passion filled faith. So much so that it stopped the King of heaven in the tracks of his own purpose and mission in the earth. Jesus stopped what He was doing and rerouted His initial intended ministry travel for that day because of this man's faith. As a result, His passion got Jesus' full attention and it compelled Him towards this man' dwelling.

> He (Jesus) entered Capernaum. And a certain centurion's servant, who was dear to him, was sick and ready to die. So when he heard about Jesus, he sent elders of the Jews to Him, pleading with Him to come and heal his servant. And when they came to Jesus, they begged Him earnestly, saying that the one for whom He should do this was deserving, "for he loves our nation, and has built us a synagogue." Then Jesus

> went with them. And when He was already not far from the house, the centurion sent friends to Him, saying to Him, "Lord, do not trouble Yourself, for I am not worthy that You should enter under my roof. Therefore I did not even think myself worthy to come to You. But say the word, and my servant will be healed. For I also am a man placed under authority, having soldiers under me. And I say to one, 'Go,' and he goes; and to another, 'Come,' and he comes; and to my servant, 'Do this,' and he does it." When Jesus heard these things, He marveled at him, and turned around and said to the crowd that followed Him, "I say to you, I have not found such great faith, not even in Israel!" And those who were sent, returning to the house, found the servant well who had been sick. (Luke 7:1-10)

Passionate faith got Jesus' attention and it compelled Him to move towards the centurion's desperate circumstance which ended up becoming a huge blessing for not only Him (his dearest servant being healed) but became a divine miracle for another. This is what passion in purpose can do. It can release blessings and miracles not just for us but it can even affect the destiny of others around us. Praise God! That's why the Lord comes and visits you by His precious Holy Spirit everyday and says, "Child of God, you know that situation you have been dealing with? You can overcome that situation. Not by your might, but by Mine. Not by your plans, but by Mine. Not by your strength, but by Mine!" Philippians 4:13 says, "I can do all things through Christ who strengthens me." I know many of you have quoted this verse since you were a child in Sunday school, but the question is, do we still have that same passionate and childlike faith when we are actually challenged to live these verses out as adults in our daily lives?

Christ really does want to strengthen us in all things. When the Bible says "all," it means ALL . Your situation, the thing that you're walking through, the thing that you're going through right now does not surprise God! When you remain steadfast and passionate about your purpose and destiny while you are going through things in life no matter how easy or difficult you give God another opportunity to show up and show off! This shows how incredible and awesome He is in and through you, but it takes passion for us to get there. God Himself is passionate too. He is passionate about you; He knows your end from your beginning. In the gospel of John 15:16 it declares a remarkable truth, "You did not choose Me, but I have chose you and appointed you that you should go and bear fruit, and that your fruit should remain, that whatever you ask the Father in My name He will give you." It is the same message from Genesis to Revelation. When God finally spoke His first words to Adam and Eve in the Old Testament, He said, "Go, be fruitful and multiply." Jesus the Son of God repeated the same Words in the New Testament when He said, "You did not choose Me; I have chosen you. Now go bear fruit." It's the same exact message. The passion that drove Jesus towards His mission and vision daily (restoring mankind back to right relationship with God) was the passion to restore God's master plan for His purposes in the earth.

So now it's time to get passionate about your own purpose and destiny too. Quit messing around with your life! Quit playing games with God! How long does it take you to do what He has asked you to do? How many burning bushes do you need? How many Red Seas do you need Him to open for you? How many years do you have to work for your Rachel (whatever that is for you) like how Jacob did for Laban before you obtain your true heart's desire? (see Genesis Chapter 29-30) It's time to become passionate or maybe re-passionate again about God's plan for your life. This is sobering, and serious! There are several of you who need to say, "God here I am; I'm going all the way with you today!" Why? Because you are making a decision to become passionate about fulfilling your purpose and destiny. Life isn't a 'game' as so many people in the world with a lack of understanding proclaim. You were born for a reason. No, it doesn't mean that you can't have fun along the way. Those who have been liberated from Christian legalism and have been serving the Lord a while know that serving Jesus is joyful. Life in God and in the Spirit is joyful. My God gives life and freedom and my passion for serving Him brings my life joy, peace, happiness, laughter, fulfillment and blessing. Your life can be like this also, but it's time to get passionate, you have a destiny to fulfill. God has a purpose and plan for your life and He is waiting to reveal what His purpose and plan is. You see, you and I existed in God's plan before we were a thought in our mother's mind or in our parents' hearts. You existed in the mind of God before you ever appeared on this earth. God Himself became passionate about you and your destiny.

> "For You formed my inward parts; You covered me in my mother's womb. I will praise you for I am fearfully and wonderfully made; marvelous are Your works, and that my soul knows very well. My frame was not hidden from You, When I was made in secret, and skillfully wrought in the lowest parts of the earth, Your eyes saw my substance being yet unformed. And in your book they all were written, the days fashioned for me when as yet there were none of them. How precious also are Your thoughts to me, O God! How great is the sum of them!" (Psalm 139:13-17)

Does your heart wither before such a prospect? Do your circumstances and limitations, your failures or weakness cause you to doubt such grand possibilities? Listen as the Lord would say to you, "If I am able to save your soul from eternal darkness and put My Spirit within you, resurrecting your soul from the impending doom of darkness and death and bring you into My Son's Kingdom of light and life, am I not able to recreate your circumstances? I have given you the breath of life and eternal hope through salvation and I am also able to create a whole new world of purpose and destiny where you live. I am the God of both grace and glory!

The grace by which I created you and gave you new life is able to now create (or re-create) your purpose and destiny, bringing new blessings to your life!"

What a powerful prophetic release of God's voice and Word over your life! It's time to get passionate about your future again, but maybe you can only see the dismal need for your marriage, the darkened condition of your home, the stressful situation at work, or the dismal nature of your influence for Christ as a leader. Or you already have the beginning sparks of romance, and you want more than the fire of passion; you want the pure flame of holy love. Maybe you have seen the ignition of fresh effectiveness at your place of business, but you want God to bring this beyond a flashy beginning and establish it with His blessing and favor on your enterprise. Or... why don't you recite your own circumstance that I haven't been able to mention or articulate here? What is the darkest situation you are facing? What is the brightest possibility you hold? In either case or in both, describe them to the Lord and let this become the beginning place for the Spirit of God to show you the pathway to realizing your life's passion – your own true purpose and destiny.

Chapter 17
The Blame Game

Be honest, how many of us play the blame game from time to time? Like how a woman in the 'push' stages of her pregnancy has a sudden supposed epiphany during her intense labor pains and shouts out "it was my husband who got me into this mess in the first place!" We too, like to blame others for the intense pain and difficulty we experience in our lives. Psalm 139:13-17 is a vital, key passage of scripture. It solves our present day identity crisis that most of us suffer with the majority of our lives. As I shared with you before, I worked in behavioral health for six years. I dealt with everything from severe schizophrenia to major depression. I have worked with, counseled, or ministered to people almost all of my life so I feel that I have a voice on this subject. The majority of people that I've worked with have an identity crisis and that is the biggest part of their problem, not necessarily some medical illness or diagnosis. They say "Well, I'm this or I'm that, or my father did this to me, or this happened to me because..." or they blame the way they are on their parents past mistakes. Now I'm not saying that some things can't affect the immediate outcome of our lives due to a chemical imbalance or physical illness, or due to another's sin against us; but what I am saying is that it doesn't have to stay like that all your life and determine the overall outcome of your destiny either.

We have been doing the blame game ever since the beginning of Creation with Adam and Eve in the Garden of Eden. When God came looking for Adam he said, "Lord, you know that woman that you gave to me? She gave me the apple and I ate it." Then when God came looking for Eve, He asked her; "What in the world happened here Eve?" She said, "Well, you know that serpent that's been slithering around here, he told me it was ok to eat it." Even as children, when our mom or dad would call me and my brother Dickie into the house after discovering our well hidden mischief (so we thought) and asked us "Ok... which one of you two did this?" We would both immediately get that puzzled stare on our faces that seemed to say, "I'm the innocent one here" and always conveniently point the blame at each other. I'm sure it must have been very comical for my parents at the time when we were young and growing up. I don't know how they ever managed to keep a straight face while punishing us two characters. Or how about when we were in school and the teacher wanted to know who blew the spit wad at the chalkboard, the blame was always (and no disrespect here) the shy and innocent nerdy looking kid on the other side of the classroom. What I am saying here is that we have learned, even as children to let someone else take our blame. We want to shift the blame onto anything else other than ourselves. The reality is this; God doesn't want you to blame-shift, He expects us to take responsibility for our irresponsibility. He wants to set you free of your identity crisis, and He wants you to understand how awesome He is and how awesome your potential is.

There's another story that the Bible tells us about someone taking the blame for others shortcomings. Jesus, the Lamb of God took our blame and He bore it all on the cross, the shame that we have been guilty of but blamed others for. He suffered and died so that we would not have that blame assigned to us. He died to bring redemption. As adults we live with regrets, and with memories that need healing, when it comes time to say, "Hey, I want you to know it was me who did this" those on earth may want to cast stones at you, but the great price that Jesus paid shifts the blame from you onto Him. You go before Him and He says sin... what sin?

> "And you He made alive, who were dead in trespasses and sins, in which you once walked according to the course of this world, according to the prince of the power of the air, the spirit who now works in the sons of disobedience, among whom also we all once conducted ourselves in the lusts of our flesh, fulfilling the desires of the flesh and of the mind, and were by nature children of wrath, just as the others, but God, who is rich in mercy, because of His great love with which He loved us, even when we were dead in trespasses, made us alive together with Christ (by grace you have been saved)..." (Ephesians 2:1-5)

> "For in Him we live, and move, and have our being..." (Acts 17:28)

In whom do we live and move? It's in Him. Our whole being (the totality of our lives past, present, future) exists only in Him. When we live in Him, we are strengthened by Him for the things that come our way. When we move in Him, we are filled with faith, joy, and peace in every situation that the world or the enemy sends our way to move us to defeat. If we remain true to Him, He is faithful to see us through all those things that bring temptation in our lives. Jesus was tempted as we are; He was offered everything, and He chose nothing but His Father's ultimate plan, purpose, and destiny for His life. You too can become so built up in Him, and come to such a place in your walk and relationship with God, where you just shake off the words of the enemy and follow after Christ as you step into His purpose and destiny for your life. Amen.

Who Will You Look Like?

When children are born, they carry different genes from the family gene pool of their birth mothers and fathers. As a result, they come out of the womb, and as they begin to grow, they start to carry different features and physical traits of their parents. In other words, they come out looking like their mother, father or a combination of them both. Who did you come out looking more like? Those of us who have been "born again" are now identified as being Christians.

Where did we even get the name Christian? It's simply because the people, who received Christ as Messiah, found Christ's life inside of them and after becoming born again, they began to not only look like but act like and reflect the very characteristics and nature of their Savior Jesus Christ Himself. All of those spiritual sons and daughters that were born into the Kingdom of God began to emulate and reflect their "birth father" Jesus Christ. Simply put, they came out of the womb of salvation looking like and acting like their Messiah Jesus. Instead of calling them "those weirdo's" or "those fanatics," they began to call them "Christ-ians" or what we believers in Jesus Christ are now called all over the world today, Christians.

The early disciples of Jesus were called Christians because they emulated the very ministry and nature of Christ's life Himself. They were actually reproducing the life and ministry of Christ in the earth. The early Messianic believers were pregnant with purpose and destiny that changed the face of the world as we know it. How many know that even today His true sons and daughters are unmistakably recognizable. We can still recognize the true Christians when we see one can't we? Why? Because they look like, and their lives reflect the character, nature, mission, and vision of Jesus Christ.

Some people just profess to be Christians with their mouths and yet others actually live out the Christian way with their lives. They are the ones that don't have to say a word with their mouths because the manifested presence of Jesus comes forth out of the things they both say and do which reveals His true nature and love to others. In the Gospel of John, Jesus describes this truth in greater detail when He is praying to the Father about His mission, purpose and destiny with those early Christians that He Himself birthed into the Kingdom of God. Let's examine His prayer:

> "I have manifested Your name to the men whom You have given Me out of the world. They were Yours, You gave them to Me, and they have kept Your word. Now they have known that all things which You have given Me are from You. For I have given to them the words which You have given Me; and they have received them, and have known surely that I came forth from You; and they have believed that You sent Me. "I pray for them. I do not pray for the world but for those whom You have given Me, for they are Yours. And all Mine are Yours, and Yours are Mine, and I am glorified in them. Now I am no longer in the world, but these are in the world, and I come to You. Holy Father, keep through Your name those whom You have given Me, that they may be one as We are. While I was with them in the world, I kept them in Your name. Those whom You gave Me I have kept; and none of them is lost except the son of perdition, that the Scripture might be fulfilled. But now I come to You, and these things I speak in the world, that they may have My joy fulfilled in themselves... "I do not pray for these alone, but also for those who will believe in Me through their word; that they all may be one, as You, Father, are in Me, and I in You; that they also

> may be one in Us, that the world may believe that You sent Me. And the glory which You gave Me I have given them, that they may be one just as We are one: I in them, and You in Me; that they may be made perfect in one, and that the world may know that You have sent Me, and have loved them as You have loved Me. "Father, I desire that they also whom You gave Me may be with Me where I am, that they may behold My glory which You have given Me; for You loved Me before the foundation of the world. O righteous Father! The world has not known You, but I have known You; and these have known that You sent Me. And I have declared to them Your name, and will declare it, that the love with which You loved Me may be in them, and I in them." (John 17:6-24)

I don't know about you, but I want to look and be more like my Jesus don't you? In ancient church history there was a revival called "The Bright and Shining Revival" where people just shined with the very presence of Christ. The Welsh Revival of 1904 is described as being like a mighty tornado. The Spirit of God swept across the land until mountains and valleys, cities and villages were filled with the mighty manifestations of God's light and presence. Churches were crowded and meetings went on day and night. Prayer, singing and testimonies would sweep over congregations in torrents and hundreds turned to the Lord. Never in the history of Wales had such indescribable scenes been witnessed. Those people didn't have to say a thing. They would walk into a store and the Christ within them, the hope of glory, and the thing that they were birthing, the thing that they were pregnant with from heaven shone out of them and people would literally call them "shining ones." The glory of Christ inside of them was revealed on the earth. Those Christians were allowing Him to be birthed through them on the earth. People would want to know what it was. They would come up and ask them; "Why are you glowing, or why are you shining?"

There was a brief season in the church that I pastor, where some of these types of things were divinely happening in our midst and among a few of our members. The Lord's presence would just come into our service or prayer meetings so thick and powerful. Some time after either the service or prayer meeting, a few people in our church would just be doing their "thing" and go to the local grocery store or gas station. People would come up to them and say something like, "My your just glowing today!" Or something like; "Did you know that you are shining?" We had been having some pretty powerful services where the presence of God was being manifested in our midst! The power of God was so thick; everyone there was just saturated with the power and presence of God! It was truly amazing, powerful, and refreshing! People had even claimed that they could smell the aroma of the presence of God. My own mother Racheal even claims to have smelled the very fragrance and essence of what Jesus smells like. These people, without even trying, went out into the communities they all lived in and began to emulate the life and light of Jesus Christ and thereby we were able to lead them to Christ right there on the spot!

Can you imagine if the church could shine that bright today as it did in the great Welsh Revival of 1904? I believe that's one of the reasons why the Lord says don't hide your light under a bushel (see Matthew 5:14-16). Like the old Sunday school song says, "This little light of mine...I'm gonna let it shine...Let it shine...let it shine...let it shine!" Where do you think we got that song? You say; "Oh, it's just a cute little song we learned when we were kids." No, there is a reason why that song was birthed on the earth. The Holy Spirit birthed it within the heart of an anointed writer because the light and life of Jesus Christ was shining out from men and woman's lives. People were coming to know the life that is the light of men. Oh, you are beginning to tap into the main vein of heavens truth here and it's where the gold nuggets are hidden!

I have a question for some of you who feel as if it is your destiny and desire to serve God in formal church ministry. Why are you going into ministry in the first place? I remember when I was young and I had just given my heart and life to Jesus Christ. I was on fire for God and it seemed as if the Bible I bought was bigger than I was. During those special years, nothing could stop my desire for more of God. I would literally run to my church every time the doors were open. I would say, "Mom, got to eat quick, and then I have to run." She would asked, "Why, where are you going, son?" Then I would say, "I have to go to church and I don't want to be late." She'd say, "This early babe?" I'd say, "Yeah, I have to get their early so I can get a good seat!" You see, like you I was hungry and thirsty for more of God, but what was driving me was the intense desire placed there by the Holy Spirit to fulfill my life's purpose and destiny. My spiritual womb was crying out. I wanted intimacy, relationship, and I wanted to know the Lord in the power of His might (see Ephesians 6:10).

Everything inside of me was saying "run to the church! Run to the front row so your destiny can get fed!" I am telling you it was there on the front row of Sweetwater Church of the Valley in Glendale, Arizona where I was impregnated in the spiritual womb of my life and destiny began to be revealed to me. After the conception of salvation in the spiritual womb of my life with the divine Seed of heaven, my life was never the same again. It wrecked me, and ruined me; it messed everything up (in a good way). You see I had my own plans for my life. My parents had their plans for my life, but it messed all of our plans up.

Whether you know it or not you are giving birth to your purpose and destiny even now! Many of you are going places in the ministry. You are going to need to recall this information when you begin to call your own spiritual sons and daughters into their purpose and destiny and into their ministry. What will that look like? What will they look like? Who will they look like? Maybe you're a person who is ready to now open up your spiritual womb. Remember as in natural pregnancy it only takes one seed to conceive. In the natural, women are giving birth as we speak, in labor and delivery rooms, in the backseat of a car, in a taxicab in New York City, in airplanes, on trains, in board rooms and in bedrooms all over the world. It is happening in every conceivable place. You can't stop it! I've learned all kinds of things about what women have to go through to give birth. They have to push in the most unlikely places. When it's time to give birth, it doesn't come with any modesty. They often times have to do it for the "world" to see. But in spite of all the craziness that follows birthing time, no matter what, every time you hear the groans and moans of a woman pushing in the act of labor say "Uhhhh!!!" followed by a little babies "Wahhh!!!" the glory of God is revealed in a life that has just been born.

Absolutely everyone has God's life breathed into them at birth, even those who say they don't believe in the very God who gave them that life. Our American soldiers that are over in the Middle East, as crazy as this may seem, there is a purpose for them being over there in that hostile region.

We have a precious long time member of our congregation by the name of Jonnie Pruitt who has been a huge supporter and blessing to our church and to my wife Phaedra, and I personally. Jonnie recently lost her son Tyler in the war on terrorism in Iraq. He joined the army and became a medic. He told his mother before he left, "Mom, I don't understand it. I just know deep down inside that I have to be over there - It's my purpose." Sometimes purpose cries out from way down on the inside of us. His mother said, "Are you sure Tyler?" He said, "Mom, I have got to be over there. It's my purpose!"

That young man went over there with that "inner knowing" and served the army and his country with great honor and with great purpose in his heart. One day while doing what he believed to be his purpose and what gave him a sense of destiny, the Taliban set up a trap for his military unit and lunched a rocket into the center of his troop and it exploded with a huge impact. Needless to say, some men lost their lives that day but Jonnie's medic son didn't just lose his life he "gave" his life so that others could have a chance at living theirs. Tyler was willing to do whatever it took to fulfill that deep "inner knowing" to complete his destiny even to the point of dying for what he felt was his purpose.

Since Tyler's death, there have been some incredible testimonies and miracles that came about as a result of this tragedy. Are you willing to follow your destiny in life, no matter the cost? Tyler Pruitt's story of mission, purpose and destiny sounds like another Son's mission that I know about in the Bible. It sounds and looks a lot like Jesus' true mission, purpose and destiny. He came to seek and save the lost, to set captives free, to heal the wounded and hurting, and to set at liberty those who are bound and afflicted. This is why we have to continue to minister to our veterans and to the ex-soldiers that are so messed up from what they have seen and heard and what they had to go through in the military. There can be many horrible things that soldiers face, but in spite of all those painful situations, God doesn't waste anything in our lives; the good, the bad, or the ugly.

There is something I want you to know that's very specific to your purpose and destiny. When Jesus came, He had a "purpose statement." He said in John 10:10-11, "The thief (Satan) does not come except to steal, and to kill, and to destroy. I (Jesus) have come that they may have life, and that they may have it more abundantly. "I am the good shepherd. The good shepherd gives His life for the sheep." Men may take lives, but Jesus always gives life. His life is everlasting, abundant, joyful, and it is blessed. I have given much of my ministry life to study this in the Greek and Hebrew text up, down, and around the Word of God. I'm telling you, it all points to the same thing: God is a life giver and He wants us to be like Him in every possible way in every area of our life and destiny so that we can emulate His life and love in all we say and do for Him. Many of us are like Tyler, but we are serving in the army of the Lord as spiritual medics in the Kingdom of God. The Bible says in John 15:13, "Greater love has no man than this, than to lay down His life for His friends." Talk about purpose and destiny. Tyler's inner purpose emulated Jesus.'

Let's go a little deeper in our study of purpose and destiny. Whenever God creates something, there's a purpose for it. Everything on this earth has a purpose and destiny connected to it in some way or another. The plants need the sun, other things need the moon. We could go on and on endlessly and talk about the glories of His Creation and how each and every part of God's Creation is linked together and has a purpose and destiny. Simply walk out your back door and look around you. All of Creation testifies of the glory of God, but as beautiful and as wonderful as all this is; still you and I are God's greatest and best creation! In Genesis1:1-29, whenever God created something unique and special in the purpose and design of the Creation of the world He would exclaim "It is good." When He created something else within that Creation, He would say the very same thing "It is good." On the sixth day, the Lord exclaimed something even better… Let's look at this:

> "In the beginning God created the heavens and the earth..."
>
> "And God saw the light, that it was good..."
>
> "And God called the dry land Earth, and the gathering together of the waters He called seas, and God saw that it was good...."
>
> "And the earth brought forth grass, the herb that yields seed according to its kind, and the tree that yields fruit, whose seed is in itself according to its king, And God saw that it was good…."
>
> "Then God made two great lights: the greater light to rule the day, and the lesser light to rule the night. He made the stars also. God set them in the firmament of the heavens to give light on the earth, and to rule over the day and over the night, and to divide the light from the darkness. And God saw that it was good..."

> "So God created great sea creatures and every living thing that moves, with which the waters abounded, according to their kind, and every winged bird according to its kind And God saw that it was good...."
>
> "And God made the beasts of the earth according to its kind, cattle according to its kind, and everything that creeps upon the earth, according to its kind And God saw that it was good...."
>
> "Then God said, Let Us make man in Our image, according to Our likeness; let them have dominion over the fish of the sea, over the birds of the air, and over the cattle, over all the earth and every creeping thing that creeps on the earth." So God created man in His own image; in the image of God He created him, male and female He created them. Then God blessed them...."

As you can plainly see, one of God's initial purposes for creating us in His image was to allow us to live in His blessing and dominion. Remember that He came to give us a blessed life; an abundant life even from the very beginning of time. I want to draw your attention to in Genesis 1:31; "Then God saw everything He had made, and indeed it was very good... So the evening and the morning were the sixth day." Seven times God said "it was good," but after God created mankind on the sixth day God declared that we were "very good."

We were the center of His Creation being fruitful, multiplying, and taking our God ordained dominion in the earth that He created for us to have dominion over. In other words, mankind was in the center of His Creation, fulfilling our God ordained purpose and destiny in the earth and it wasn't just good to God; it was very good. Yes, all of Creation testifies that God is indeed good and wonderful, but it wasn't until God created man after His own image, male and female, did He use the words "very good" concerning everything He had created. Yes, we are very good in God's eyes! It was our Father's way of saying "I approve!" It was His way of saying, "I think the babies I made look very good in my sight and I am a proud Father, and look, they even look just like Us!" Do these words sound familiar? Maybe they sound similar to the words that you spoke out when you first saw your children born. They looked so beautifully perfect to you. There was no flaw in them in your eyes because all you saw was what you and your spouse had made together. You saw the "Us" (the two of you) in them. This is a powerful truth to know and something so important to implant deep within our spiritual understanding as this is a practical way to see the triune nature of God; each different, and unique, part of you contained in one form – your child.

I also want you to note how many times the scripture says in Genesis Chapter 1 that He (God) created things after their "own kind," but we were created in His image. In the image and likeness of our Father God! God instituted divine order, government, and laws in Creation so that man could be blessed and take dominion in their purpose and destiny. This is not so we can just be fruitful and multiply, and have a bunch of kids on the earth! NO! There is a greater purpose for this. The Lord said, "Be fruitful and multiply" so that we can have dominion over all the things that He has created because He's deposited Himself in each of us. The "He" in "you" can settle for nothing less than dominion. The Lord is saying, "I've blessed you; now go take your dominion with the authority I placed inside of you when I created you. I have given it to you and I will bless you, and in that blessing you can take full dominion with what I have called you and blessed you to do and to be in your purpose and destiny as My sons and daughters in My image and likeness."

I want to share a purpose and destiny story the Lord showed my mother Racheal from her backyard garden. One sunny spring day she was in her garden in her backyard praying and seeking the Lord admiring an apple tree that she had planted a while back and was so proud of how well it was growing when all of a sudden the Holy Spirit began to open the eyes of her understanding. As she was standing there gazing at this tree, she began to see this tree's potential and saw how it was pregnant with purpose. It was budding pretty white flowers and was starting to grow tiny apples underneath the buds. She is standing there thinking about these things and the Holy Spirit speaks gently to her heart and says, "See Racheal, the blossoms are there and they are beginning to bloom, along with all the honey bees doing their part with cross pollination." And all of a sudden she begins to look at that tree with eyes of purpose and destiny. Then the Holy Spirit spoke to heart again; "The stem that the blossoms are attached to is pregnant with its purpose even as small as they are now. The blossoms will die out, but the stem will soon produce large ripe green apples. That is what I created it to do. That is its purpose and destiny." Then the Holy Spirit urged her to observe her grapefruit tree that also had blossoms attached to its' stems, the two trees were the same (both fruit trees) yet very different. Their blossoms were different. The colors of the leaves were different as were the shape and size as well as the fruit they would ultimately produce. Everything was growing, being birthed and created after its' own kind; right there in her own backyard. Yes, both were fruit trees with similar yet two very distinct purposes.

A few weeks later I had come over to her house to visit. She and my dad showed me the beautiful apple tree in their backyard where my mother began to tell me her revelation. I noticed from both fruits that she showed me that the apple leaf, blossom, and stem were entirely different than the same growth on the grapefruit tree. Even when you smelled them both they smelled very different from one another. Now I know it doesn't take great prophetic discernment or a college education to know that the purpose and destiny of an apple tree, even from a seed, is to produce ripe green apples. I just want to thank my mother right now for sharing what the Lord had revealed to her by the Spirit of God that day in such a pure way. You see, that beautiful green apple beginning to grow on her tree was truly there for a purpose.

You see, we are all unique and different. Not one of us are the same. We're all different, each in our own way. We look different, act different and we have different color skin. We are all unique after our own kind. Even our fingerprints are all unique, they're all different. Your fingerprints are like the signature of God upon your life. Like how a master artist signs their signature upon their creative work to signify that piece of artwork is an original from its creator. So too, your very fingerprints testify that you are an original creative piece of God's handiwork. Fingerprints tell us we are not alike; we each have a different purpose to fulfill. We are all blossoming and becoming pregnant with purpose and destiny in different ways. We need to take dominion along the way as He told us to do all along. We need to be fruitful and multiply, in the Spirit and in the natural, subduing and taking as much dominion before we leave this place and go into eternity. What are you uniquely designed for? What are you called to do? If someone were to take all the limits off of you, what would you do for Him?

Chapter 18
Shot Into Your Mothers Womb

> "Behold, children are a heritage from the LORD, The fruit of the womb is a reward. Like arrows in the hand of a warrior, so are the children of one's youth. Happy is the man who has his quiver full of them; they shall not be ashamed, But shall speak with their enemies in the gate." (Psalm 127:3-5)

Children are your heritage. As the Bible declares, they are like arrows in a hand of a warrior. In this case, the warrior is the Lord of Hosts. This particular passage also describes the fruit of the womb (children) being a great reward. I remember when my brother Dickie and I were little kids, we would pretend and play all the war stuff like army men, cowboys and Indians, space wars with aliens from another planet etc. While playing those different pretend games we would throw dirt clods at each other from one big hill to the other in an empty housing lot down the street from where we grew up. Then being the mischievous children that we were, we would team up, take careful aim and hurl each of our dirt clods at the same time at the neighbor kids and knock them off the other dirt hill.

This story reminded me of how a skillful archer never fires his arrows until he takes careful aim. How many know that when a skilled archer or warrior pulls back the bow, he does it with purpose and he does not miss. I've been taught how to hunt and to shoot a bow and arrow by (in my opinion) one of the best. One of my Assistant Pastor's, Ken Converse is a true outdoorsman and my armor bearer and friend. He has taken on the "interesting task" of teaching me how to hunt and shoot. Kenny is a real man's man and, needless to say, he has a lot of weapons to go with his spiritual duty of armor bearer. If you need anything to hunt with, he's got it.

Not too long ago he was patiently teaching me on a very memorable camping trip, up in Northern Arizona, how to become a skilled marksman with the bow and arrow. Just before we left for this trip I had received a personal prophecy over my life. It said I was a bow in the hands of God and God was going to give me sharp prophetic arrows (special words from the Lord to release). It also said that as the Lord through the Holy Spirit began to pull back on my prophetic gift I would become a skilled archer in the hands of the Lord as a voice to His people. The Holy Spirit would begin to pull back my gift (the bow) and let go of His sharp arrows (prophetic words) and hit the intended targets of His people. I thought that word over my life was pretty cool because I've always wanted to shoot a bow and arrow. When a skilled archer pulls back the bow, he does it with purpose. An archer doesn't just pull back the bow and not aim at anything. In war, he pulls it back and takes careful aim at what he's shooting at whatever it may be, either practice target, enemy, or game. He does not let go of the tension of the break on the bow until he has reached careful aim and then he releases. A skilled archer intends to hit the target and aims carefully.

While we were up in the mountains messing around with targets, I thought to myself, I can do this, "Pastor Kenny, give me that bow."

I tried his bow, but Pastor Kenny is very strong. He gave me his bow and I pulled... uhhhh... and couldn't get the bow to break (couldn't pull the wire on the bow back far enough to release it properly because of the tension). Then I pulled again... uhhh... Kenny's bow is a compound bow, they have a draw blade, it's calculated, and they have a drop weight on them. You can adjust them and set them at different draw pulls for different things. Kenny's bow is set at 65 lbs. It's a pretty strong pull and once you get it up into aiming eyesight, it breaks and then you release it. You can hold it out there but it still has a lot of weight set on it. So, I pulled one last time and was finally able to get it back, holding my breath I set the arrow on its mark and released it, then I could breathe. It fired straight and fast, the arrow shot through the air with great speed. I did that a few more times and after that I gained a lot of confidence, it almost felt natural for me. Then there was the importance of taking careful aim. The first few times I was aiming at the target the arrows were going wild and way out in front of or beyond the target. I was just thankful everyone was a clear distance away from me as the next few arrows I pulled back and shot would hit the ground and skid across the field where we were standing. Then we had to go and hunt down all the arrows I shot because at that speed they would get buried in the dirt and foliage. Finally, I said, "Kenny, are you sure you want to teach me to do this?" Seriously, I had that prophetic word inside of me, and I really wanted to learn this so I was hoping that he was still up for the task after watching my first few horrible shots. It wasn't long, just a few more pulls, and I started getting the hang of it. I was hitting the target, honestly, dead center every time even from a significant distance away! Pastor Kenny started to look at what I was doing in amazement and began to say things like, "Ahhhh... that was beginner's luck" and laugh. Then Kenny would try to shoot and he would come close to or land on the target but not hit the mark. To be honest with you I gloated a little about that and I was becoming more excited as I was thinking to myself "Wow, now here is the master hunter guy and

I'm whopping him!"

You see, our children that we have given birth to (or will give birth to in the future) and the things we are birthing as it relates to our purpose and destiny in the Lord are like a bow and an arrow in the hands of a skilled archer. When God took you out of His heavenly quiver, He was ready to shoot you out as a skilled archer out of time, space, and eternity. God pulled back His divine bow of purpose and destiny and shot you out like a sharp arrow into the earth, and the Lord of all Creation is not going to miss. He is going to hit His target every time! The mark or the bull's eye was your mother's womb. When you were born, He hit His target. Like a skilled archer, you were shot out like an arrow out of heaven into your mother's womb for a purpose. Praise God! That is so powerful! Do you know what a quiver is? It's what skilled archers use to contain and carry all their arrows. Psalm 127:5 says, "Happy is the man who has his quiver full..." Gods quiver is full of purpose and destiny and His reward and delight was when He reached back into His quiver and shot you out into the earth from heaven and He hit the mark – your mother's womb and you were born!

I pray that I have been like a skilled archer prophetically. I know nothing about each of you personally, or what you may be going through, but I have been able to release God's Word to you like a divine bow and sharp arrow. I have helped you by hitting the mark; helping you better understand and discover your life's purpose and destiny. I pray that I am ministering to you and hitting the mark of your heart. My prayer is that you are getting impregnated with what you're called to do. You are an arrow in the hands of a skilled archer and He (the Lord) never misses. When God, in His perfect timing, releases you into your true purpose and destiny, His arrow will hit the mark in your life. Discovering and fulfilling your purpose and destiny will not just become a reward for you in this life, but it will also be a reward for you in the next. When you discover and truly fulfill your purpose and destiny, it becomes a delight to your Father God. When the Lord pulled you from His heavenly quiver He literally pulled you out of His creative genius, out from eternity, and at that very moment released your potential into the earth with His backing. When you absorb this into your spirit each day it becomes more and more valuable.

As we get older, we naturally begin to start thinking more seriously about what we did with our lives. We begin to think about our future more; often times a little too late. Don't wait until then, start thinking about it now. God wants to use you right here and now; no matter how old or how young you may be. It's never too late to begin your journey of destiny in the Lord. What was God skillfully aiming at when He released you from heaven? Well, if the fruit of the womb is a reward, your birth is the act of God rewarding Himself. He shot you out from the realms of eternity and into a very specific time. He used a specific route and aimed for a specific target; that target was your momma's womb. You became His child when you were released from your mother's womb. When you became a living being you were another child – an arrow from the Father's quiver that hit the mark of purpose and destiny in the earth, and the day you gave your heart and life to Jesus Christ spiritually you became a son or daughter, a child of God shot forth from His quiver into the Kingdom of God. Thank you Jesus!

Born to Take Divine Authority

God always operates with a Triune nature: the Father, Son, and the Holy Spirit. God is a God of purpose and He is a God of plan, design, and timing. God loves to mess with our timing. Why? Because when we rely on, depend on, or work in our own timing, too often we try to take the credit for what God is actually doing in our lives. I believe that God does, says, and creates nothing beyond these three perimeters. When God created you and me, He did so deliberately, as a part of a

Master Plan with a unique design to meet His own strategic objectives and appointments for our lives in our time. In Jeremiah 1:5 you will find foundational scriptures for this entire teaching. Remember it says that, "Before I formed you in the womb I knew you…." So what is God really saying? He is saying that He has a plan for everyone; yes, even the people who are without Christ on this earth, and that is that God has a plan for them to discover their true life in Christ. He desires for everyone to know and understand what He has pre-ordained for them to do and to be in this life. If you'll notice, the question is instilled on the inside of every single one of us. "What am I here for? There must be something more than this." We try to fill up our emptiness outside of Jesus, with everything under the sun rather than with God.

A National Geographic story was showing some horrible things going on in Africa that people are doing to themselves right now to fill up the void and emptiness of their lives like self-mutilating their own bodies to try to discover something supernatural. There is a huge voodoo movement going on in that country right now. This movement is probably designed and intended by Satan to combat the huge spiritual revival and citywide transformation that is taking place over there by the power of the Holy Spirit for the Kingdom of God. Whatever the demonic motive, there is a group of people over there trying to cast different voodoo spells and incantations over their lives to gain favor or to be blessed by the spirits in the netherworld. In their ignorance without the God of truth working on their behalf, they are trying to understand things way beyond themselves. They are trying to fill the void but all they are doing is being deceived and believing a lie. Sadly, what they are engaging in to be blessed is unfortunately the very thing that is possessing them! It is skewed and demonic, ugly and perverted, because that's the enemy's plan. His plan is to pervert the truth and mess up God's intended plan and purpose for people's lives. Remember, that Satan understands the heavenly realm because he once had a position in heaven before his fall. The Bible declares that when he was cast out of heaven he fell like lightning to the earth, nevertheless, Satan still has an understanding of things in the heavenly dimension. According to the Bible, the devil even knows how to present himself before God with the other sons of God (angelic beings) with accusations concerning the servants of God.

> "Again there was a day when the sons of God came to present themselves before the LORD, and Satan came also among them to present himself before the LORD. And the LORD said to Satan, "From where do you come?" Satan answered the LORD and said, "From going to and fro on the earth, and from walking back and forth on it." Then the LORD said to Satan, "Have you considered My servant Job, that there is none like him on the earth, a blameless and upright man, one who fears God and shuns evil? And still he holds fast to his integrity, although you incited Me against him, to destroy him without cause." (Job 2:1-3)

As we can see, Satan presents a case for our disqualification with accusations against us, but through the blood of Jesus, we have redemption and sanctification working on our behalf. That life far exceeds anything that any dark power can ever create! That's why the Bible says, "No weapon formed against you shall prosper, and every tongue which rises against you in judgment you shall condemn. This is the heritage of the servants of the Lord." (Isaiah 54:17) With all that said, the Bible also declares, "Behold, I give you the authority to trample on serpents and scorpions, and over all the power of the enemy, and nothing shall by any means hurt you." (Luke 10:19) God is not only supernaturally protecting us, but He has created us to take dominion, and to operate in our divine authority in the earth. What do you do when you come against the spirits of darkness, the demonic minions, the dark realms, and forces? You take authority, dominion, and you declare, "You cannot have possession over this area or this person In Jesus Name!" You take your God given authority in Christ. When people begin to mess around in the spiritual dimension without the blood of Christ and the backing and truth of heaven working on their behalf they are liable to get messed up! That's why those demons tore up those guys called the seven sons of Sceva:

> "Then some of the itinerant Jewish exorcists took it upon themselves to call the name of the Lord Jesus over those who had evil spirits, saying, "We exorcise you by the Jesus whom Paul preaches." Also there were seven sons of Sceva, a Jewish chief priest, who did so. And the evil spirit answered and said, "Jesus I know, and Paul I know; but who are you?" Then the man in whom the evil spirit was leaped on them, overpowered them, and prevailed against them, so that they fled out of that house naked and wounded." (Acts 19:13-17)

As you can see, it's very important to know who you are in your purpose and destiny. Do you know who you are in Christ? Do you know who He is in you? Better yet, try this one – does the kingdom of darkness know who you are? Is the realm of darkness saying this about you: "Jesus I know, Paul I know; but who are you?" Listen, you had better know your divine purpose when you start dealing with demons, demonic forces, and minions of the devil, wizards, witches, voodoo priestesses and all those other demonic principalities; you had better know about that life and power on the inside of you! You had better know your authority, and know you can take dominion! Jesus said in Mark 16:17, "And these signs shall follow those who believe: In My name they shall cast out demons...." Jesus told us how to take our authority and dominion in Mark 11:23-24: "For assuredly, I say to you, whosoever says to this mountain, 'Be removed and be cast into the sea," and does not doubt in his heart, but believes that those things he says will be done, he will have whatever he says. Therefore I say to you, whatever things you ask when you pray, believe that you receive them, and you will have them." Do you want to operate in that kind of dominion and authority? I don't want to go out of this world and into the next until I've experienced everything in His kingdom on earth!

Everybody seems to be waiting for their kingdom in heaven and their sweet mansion in the sky when they die, but don't you see, the Father wants to bring His Kingdom here on earth. Even when Jesus taught us how to pray, He used this description of the dominion plan: "Your Kingdom come. Your will be done On earth as it is in heaven." (Matthew 6:10) When Jesus comes back again, He's bringing His Kingdom here on earth. The Bible says this; He is bringing the Kingdom to the earth for a thousand years. Halleluiah! I want to be ready, don't you? I want to know where I fit in the Master's plan, don't you? I do know this, I am a skilled archer in the hands of the Lord. I now know that I can pull a bow with prophetic arrows and with His anointing and His help, I can hit the mark! I'm not just living in a pretend world any longer, but I'm an arrow in the hands of a skilled archer! Who are you child of God?

Chapter 19
Spiritual Endometriosis

Your God-given dreams are not religious options, but they are prophetic imperatives. The Apostle John says this about Jesus' purpose and destiny in the earth in John 17:4, "I have glorified You on the earth. I have finished the work which You have given me to do." Purpose is a very specific work that God has assigned for each of us to do. Jesus is our chief example in all things, and if He glorified God by finishing the work the Father gave Him to do by fulfilling His purpose in the earth, then we can do the very same thing with our life too! Jesus' work and destiny was to seek and save the lost, and the lost always came looking for Him. Guess what, they still do today! Because I have such a high value on life, I believe that it's a sin for a person to take their own life. Our life is not ours' to take. The Lord is the Author, the giver, and finisher of life, Amen.

Recently a man called the church office who desired to take his own life, which could have aborted his purpose and destiny. I was thinking about this whole scenario and how an answered phone call from a staff member at our church got a call from a man in crisis that day. In a split moment, that call become an event in the grand scheme of that staff person's life purpose and destiny. Our staffer was able to help prevent a tragedy like this from taking place and seeing another precious person's destiny in the earth cut short and wasted. I was blown away by the revelation that this person was born for that very moment in time to answer the phone to help counsel that man through the snare of Satan's destructive scheme. That call not only turned into saving that man's life from being cut short but it also worked toward saving another person's true purpose and destiny from being cut short. Again, it's not within our power to take our own life, but it is within our power to save a life.

> "For My thoughts are not your thoughts, nor are your ways My ways," says the Lord. "For as the heavens are higher than the earth, so are My ways higher than your ways, and my thoughts than your thoughts." (Isaiah 55:8-9)

> "For I know the thoughts that I think toward you, says the Lord, thoughts of peace, and not of evil, to give you a future and a hope." (Jeremiah 29:11)

Eternal life is our hope; we are not ashamed. The future is all about purpose, dominion, and authority. It's about advancing the Kingdom of God with our life. It's about saying at the end of our life, as Jesus was able to say, "I've finished the work that you've given me to do." Some of us are so busy trying to figure this all out that we're missing the simple and the obvious. Some of you are too heavenly minded to be any earthly good, and some of you are so earthly minded with your head hanging low to the earth that you can't even see the heavens to experience it. Don't get hung up on theology, it isn't all about doctrine. Your life is vitally important and the earth is waiting for your life's purpose and destiny to be born. Some of you haven't become pregnant with your purpose yet because either you or something else keeps trying to attack the seed that comes to impregnate you. This is like a woman who cannot get pregnant because the chemicals and acids in her own body attack the seed and cause it to die before conception can occur. In medical terminology, it's called endometriosis.

My precious wife Phaedra suffered with this medical condition in her body for many years and it caused a lot of physical pain and emotional grief. There are some of you reading this destiny book that have been suffering with spiritual endometriosis for many years as well. Your past hurts disappointments, failures and heartaches, and maybe things that people have done to you relationally or physically, have caused a scarring in the spiritual womb of your life and now spiritual endometriosis has grown all over the inside of you, and has caused you much pain and grief. Whenever God tries to shoot His destiny arrows inside of your heart you can't get impregnated because of the toxins and acid you have on the inside of your heart that kills the chance at true life.

My wife had to go in for laser surgery in the natural for this condition. She didn't realize it for such a long time but she had endometriosis all over the inside of her reproductive organs that was affecting her ability to reproduce and have children. Just like the seriousness of her natural problem, this can become as serious in the spiritual realm as well. She submitted to a laser procedure that basically burned out all of the scar tissue, harmful lesions and growth that was causing her such pain and grief. Again, this is so serious! Some people can even cause their own miscarriages if they are not careful. It's just like how a woman's body can attack their own eggs and then cancel out the possibility of those eggs being fertilized. Some people are allowing their past hurts, pains, and lack of forgiveness to give them spiritual endometriosis. God can heal you of both natural and spiritual endometriosis; submit to the laser of the Holy Spirit and let Him burn it out of you. Don't avoid the process of the procedure or it will just keep getting worse. Like the physical malady in a woman's body it will keep spreading all over the inside of your spiritual womb (your heart) and eventually it will completely take you over. I want you to know that with just one choice, with one act of immediate obedience, the healing balm of Gilead can come inside your spiritual womb, and like a medical laser, the Word of God can burn it out of you and renew and restore your chances of fertilization again.

God is trying to orchestrate divine connections that will connect you to that purpose and destiny He has for you. God is trying to speak to you every day; keep your eyes open for your prophetic signs. These signs are so vitally important to your destiny discovery. Yes, you might just be going about your business and God will divinely put you in the path of someone to speak into your destiny. Let God interrupt your day, and let the light of heaven shine upon you.

Some of you are still operating with an old burden and the Lord is going to wipe that old burden away and give you a new burden for this season. Some of you are going to have to let go of the old things of the past to receive the new things of God for today. Luke 5:37 says, "You cannot put new wine into old wineskins" so you need to prepare your spiritual womb to become a new wineskin. Allow Him to create in you a new wineskin that will hold the new wine. God is doing things uniquely and differently. It is an exciting time to be preparing for your purpose and destiny. What do you think God really thinks of you? Many of you already know that He thinks good thoughts toward you, but the real truth here is that He wants to give you a "hope" and a "future." God was thinking about this for us even in the very beginning of time. He was already thinking about your birth in this generation of time. I really want that truth to soak in, and to minister life to you. You see, everything that the Father and Jesus touched from the very beginning brought life. Everything that the Holy Spirit touches then and now brings life. There is a redemptive purpose in everything, God wants to bring everything back to Himself and restore it, and make it pure and holy. He wants to make it righteous and worthy and worth living for, and this is what He wants to do for your life right here and now!

God Can Do Anything...

Have you ever asked yourself the question "Why would God ever want to use me?" I remember when I was first saved and the Lord began to call me, and pastors began to prophesy over me and to speak over my life. I remember in those times when that clarion call, was so strong over me. A clarion call is a powerful request for action or an irresistible mandate upon one's life to fulfill their life's purpose and destiny. When this began to happen in my own life, I would go to the Lord and say, "Lord, why would you ever want to use me?" This is an important question.

Most Christians believe in an Omnipotent and Almighty God. We believe that God can do anything, we confess there are no limits to what God can do, we decree and declare it. We not only say that we know it but we quote the famous verse in Matthew 17 where Jesus was saying, "There is nothing impossible to those who believe." We believe that He can heal the sick and deliver people from demonic oppression. We believe He can cleanse the leper and He can even raise the dead. We believe He can overthrow the Pharaohs of this world. We believe if we call on the Lord, He will come and heal our land. However, even though most of us believe that, isn't it ironic that most of us cannot even believe that God can use us in the process; we can't even believe that God is big enough to use us even through all of our stuff. We might use the excuse that "He can, but He wouldn't through me, or He might use someone a little more intelligent, a little cleaner, or sharper, or certainly more talented, more charismatic, or an outgoing personality type, but certainly not me." How many of you have had these thoughts? We believe that God can do absolutely anything, but when it comes to doing something great through us, we withdraw and pull back. Do you remember when the Lord came and called Moses? What is the first thing that Moses said to God? "Lord, you can't use me." What was Moses' main excuse do you remember from scripture?

> "Then Moses said to the Lord, "O my Lord, I am not eloquent, neither before nor since You have spoken to Your servant; but I am slow of speech and slow of tongue. So the Lord said to him, "Who has made Man's mouth? Or who makes the mute, the deaf, the seeing, or the blind? Have not I, the Lord? Now therefore, go, and I will be with your mouth and teach you what you shall say." (Exodus 4:10-12)

Moses' excuse was his speech. He said to the Lord; "I'm not a good speaker - I can't talk well." And the Lord rebuked him. Moses was insulting the Lord, God Almighty, Creator of heaven and earth, the God who was, and is, and is to come. He was the God who decided to manifest Himself through a burning bush to Moses and say, "Moses, here is your purpose and destiny – your very reason for being born – the very reason for living. I want to use you – there is a whole nation in bondage and I want to use you to deliver them." Can you imagine that? That bush was burning. There was no smoke or withering. Then for the God of heaven and earth to say, "I'm going to use you to deliver My people from bondage."

And then for Moses to say back "Lord, are you sure you've got the right guy?" It was insulting to the Lord. Moses' excuse was, "I am slow of speech and slow of tongue." Many Bible scholars believe that this means that Moses stuttered, he had a speech impediment, or a stuttering problem. We see Hollywood's portrayal of Moses as this confident and together kind of guy, but Moses was a man with a stammering tongue. He would start to say something and struggle getting it out. In spite of the obvious weakness, Moses was facing, the Lord told him not to tell Him how to pick those in whom He wanted to use and show His power through. God told him that He would be his lips and speak for him.

In like manner the Apostle Paul declares this statement about his own speech; "I don't come with flattering words, eloquence of speech, but

I come with the power of the Holy Spirit the anointing of God." (I Corinthians 2:1-3). What was so ironic about this statement was that Paul was indeed a very educated man, a man who did speak eloquently as a member of the Sanhedrin – a high Jewish leader of his day. His position demanded that he be wise, knowledgeable, and skilled in the torah. Yet, here is this brilliant mind saying, "I don't come with flattering words, eloquence of speech..." He was saying that his own knowledge, understanding, talents, and abilities were nothing compared to the special way God would use him in the power of the Spirit.

Then there are those who say, "Lord, you can't use me because of my past. Don't you remember what kind of person I was? Do you remember the dark places I hung out, and all the things I've done? You can't use me! No, Lord, you want to use a more intelligent person; a person of honor." Let me remind you that all the great men and women of the Bible, every single one of them from Genesis to Revelation, all of our faith heroes were flawed just like you and I.

As I began to study God's word to counter this classic "but God can't use me because..." excuse that men so often use, the Holy Spirit meticulously went over certain facts in these Bible heroes lives; things that would only tarnish an otherwise glossy reputation. For example, Noah got drunk. We hear about all the great successes of Noah, but he liked his alcohol. Then there's Abraham, he lied about his wife Sarah to a King. What about Samson? Samson's testimony was compromised many times for some young, beautiful woman. One day he took that compromise right to the very edge, and the secret of his strength was revealed and he lost his vision. Moses disobeyed; Joshua didn't teach his children; Samuel's children were backslidden; David committed both adultery and murder; Elijah sulked and suffered with depression; Jeremiah quit the ministry; Peter denied he ever knew Jesus; not once, but three times. The Bible tells us repeatedly that these great faith heroes were not just men of integrity and great victory, but they also had some things they had to deal with in their lives.

You see, it was those very things that they all struggled with that brought forth character and integrity in their lives. It was God wanting to take someone weak and make them strong in Him.

It's important that we don't just accept people for their gifting, but for the character in their gifting. This is a problem in the church today. That's why we're seeing so many new headlines about great men and women of the faith falling and having moral failures and other difficult problems. We have overlooked some things God wants us to see. We make it acceptable because they have such powerful anointing and gifts operating in their life, but there is no character that follows their anointing. Someone could be very anointed for healing, for worship, or in prophecy, and yet, as soon as that anointing lifts from them, their life does not line up with what they just ministered.

Recently my heart broke for one of the great faith heroes of our day. I was reading an article about some of the great charismatic revivalists of the church and it was exposed as a tragedy that this man (his name is not important) was having homosexual relations and getting drunk while away from his public pulpit ministry. While he was in the anointing and operating in his calling and gifting he would prophecy about world events one day and then it seemed as if those prophecies would happen within the next few weeks or so. Yet, the people in his ministry association who would find out about his indiscretions would just overlook the character for the gifting.

Church, this is a new day, we cannot do that anymore. If you intend on ministering for the Lord, your life must line up with your gifting. It doesn't matter how gifted or talented you are, if your character and your integrity does not line up, it's not worth much in the Kingdom. You could spend forty years building up the Kingdom, years of giving your life, and with one act of disobedience that is somehow revealed to the public, it will all come toppling down. Believe me, the devil is cunning, he'll get it out. He'll find a way and he will expose you, he is the accuser of the brethren, and with one act, he can tear down years of ministry that had been built up and like Samson you can lose your eyesight (your strength and vision) and become a slave to all your enemies. Don't forget that you cannot hide anything from the Lord. What you do in secret, is not a secret from Him.

I don't even pretend to be perfect. My wife, my family, and those closest to me can tell you that I still have some things I deal with, but I am doing my best to have my character line up with my gifting. That is what was happening with these great faith heroes of old. God was trying to get their character and their integrity to line up with their calling, their plan, purpose, and their destiny. Like the great men and women of old, God may be working heavily, and harshly on something in your life so He can get you ready to fulfill His purposes in you, but some of you aren't there yet because you've been resisting His work in that particular area of your life. The Lord is not going to allow you to advance, be promoted, or move into that calling until He deals with what is going on in your life. You see, He knows that your actions are going to affect others.

As Pastor Phaedra and I are leaders in our own community, we are aware of how many eyes are upon us. It's a heavy calling. A lot of the time, you're under the microscope. You know, that's why I believe in being transparent. If I let my congregation in on my life, then they know, and they don't easily place me on a pedestal and have a false perception of me. When we become transparent with them, we become real to them and they see that we are not these perfect Godly people that can do no wrong. Often times, we are just like they are, we are being worked on and changed daily as they themselves are. Then they know how to encourage me, pray for me, and when I am struggling with something then they can help me walk through these things.

We need to be transparent today, future leaders. It doesn't mean you tell them everything, all your stuff, but be transparent. Let there be some man (for men) or woman (for women) in your life, people you know, love, and trust, that you can share some of your intimate details with. But, don't just trust anybody, however, I've learned the hard way. You need people in your life that you can be real with, so when the accuser of the brethren comes, you have witnesses to your walk. You have a couple real credible brothers or sisters who can say, "Hey, I know this man's life. You can't accuse him of this or that because I know their fruit and their character and integrity in the matter." You shut the accuser down.

It's the same thing the enemy did when he brought accusations against his servant Job. He said, "Have you considered Job?" The Lord said, "Yes, I have." He knew Job's life. So Satan threw that back at God and said, "Your hand, and hedge of protection is upon him, You've really blessed him and that's why he serves You, but if you allow me to take away all of that...." What Satan didn't perceive, is that Job's faith helped him to walk through that whole test to get to the other side of it where his purpose, destiny, and his victory laid in wait. On the other side of his test was the double blessing. Job received double for his trouble.

There's a reason why the scripture so meticulously goes over the shortcomings and the faults, and failures of its key players. Why is that? Well, plainly, it's clear the Bible is not all about them, rather, it's all about Jesus. It's all about the plan of God. It's about His Kingdom come, His will be done, on earth as it is in heaven.

How's He going to accomplish that? Through you and me flawed faith heroes. His portrait is painted in the Old Testament so we can recognize the Person in the New Testament. He is concealed in the Old Testament, but He is revealed in the New Testament. Jesus is the only One who emerges from scripture without spot, or blemish. Scripture says in Ephesians 5:27 that, He (Jesus) is coming back for a bride without "spot or wrinkle..." How's He going to do that? This is so important for you and for future generations to know. This answer is posed to you in a new question: "Who is living on the inside of you? What is the only good thing that emerges from your life and found on the inside of you? It's Jesus! He's the only good thing found in us and in our flesh.

> "For I know that in me (that is, in my flesh) nothing good dwells; for to will is present with me, but how to perform what is good I do not find." (Romans 7:18)

> "The mystery which has been hidden from ages and from generations, but now has been revealed to His saints. To them God willed to make known what are the riches of the glory of this mystery among the Gentiles: which is Christ in you, the hope of glory." (Colossians 1:26-27)

What is the hope of glory? Christ within us is. How is the Lord going to come back for a church without spot or wrinkle? The Christ within us is manifested through His Church. It's not through our good works or our many good deeds, but through us, His body, and His Church that Christ emerges without spot or wrinkle. Scriptures mar the reputations of its action heroes for a reason. They talk about their personal shortcomings, their faults, and failures. Why? Because they begin to reveal to us the redemptive purpose and plan God has for all of our lives. The Lord God has an awesome part for us to play in His Master Plan and He doesn't want us to quit dreaming about that Master Plan, because of all of our, faults, failures and mistakes.

It's very much like how a woman, who at a young age, made some poor choices, and wrong decisions about giving up her virginity before marriage. How many of you (men & women) at a young age have done something like this? You made some poor choices and some wrong decisions in this area of your life.

There are many young women who have made poor choices in the area of purity, and as a result, have lost their virginity to some smooth talking, hormonal young Casanova. Then they find themselves pregnant, walking through their pregnancy abandoned and feeling alone. I can't tell you how many women my wife and I have met as Pastors that have this type of scenario as part of their testimony and have had to walk out this kind of difficult situation. As difficult as it can be, when a young woman becomes pregnant out of wedlock and makes the choice to not abort but keep her baby, after she delivers that baby, she is blessed. Most women only see the beauty, the worth, and the potential of that child in their mind's eye. I say most, because there are some who make another choice that is always regrettable, it's called abortion.

Abortion is running ramped in this country and all future leaders need to stand up against it in love, and make your voice heard even behind the pulpit and declare that there are other options and choices to make. We need to stop this sin of killing babies in America. Praise God for those who make the right choice not to commit this horrendous act and choose to give the child growing and developing within them an opportunity to encounter the life that God intended for them to have.

We had one such young lady in our own congregation by the name of Tiesha. She got pregnant as a young teenager in high school. She was the daughter of very good deacon family in our church, a precious girl with her whole future ahead of her, and then all of a sudden due to poor choices about engaging in a sexual relationship with a young man she found herself pregnant and feeling alone. When confronted with whether to keep the baby or having an abortion, she made a right choice. Her family and her church family gathered around her, we all encouraged her and walked with her through the process. During the most difficult time of Tiesha's pregnancy our youth group also rallied around her and helped her to feel welcomed and accepted as a teen mother in the youth group, even to the point of helping her with the baby during youth meetings and special events.

Now she is living a life of victory because she made the right choice to trust God and to keep her baby. When she finally gave birth to William, he was a beautiful sweet baby. That happened a few years ago now and I am happy to say that baby was not a mistake. He gives his mother and grandparents such great joy and he has turned into a very special young man who loves the Lord with all of his heart. Whenever I see him at church, I just want to grab him up and hug him. He loves to praise and worship in church and is also found in every service singing and shouting out a loud "Praise the Lord!" When I am preaching and he is in the sanctuary, he shouts out loud "Amen Pastor Brian!" It's the cutest thing and it gets everyone in the church stirred up when they hear it. I am told that he even practices preaching little sermons at home in his room to all his stuffed animals.

You see William was worth it all! She didn't view him as something that needed to be disposed of and discarded. She viewed him as something beautiful and significant; something wonderful. She saw her child as we all did: having potential. She was brave and made the right choice to keep her baby and not abort her mistake or try to cover up her sin. With a lot of help, she became a loving mother that gave her child a chance at living out his life's purpose and destiny. Tiesha chose to allow God and others to cover her mistake with love. The Bible says in Proverbs 10:12 that, "love covers a multitude of sin."

Listen ladies, maybe you are in the very same predicament as Tiesha. When you make the right choice to keep and to finally have that child, believe me, when that child is finally born and you first lay your eyes on that precious newborn, you won't view that child as a mistake, a poor choice, or a wrong decision. You will view that baby as a bundle of joy – as a blessing from God, with potential and purpose. You will view that child how God views him - as Yours! We can never allow our own personal sins, shortcomings, and failures to steal our faith in God's redemptive purpose and plan for our lives. If I were to give in to that kind of stuff, I wouldn't be here today. There were a few times my mistakes, like in a boxing match, almost knocked me down for the count, but I've kept on getting up and fighting back. I've kept on repenting, praying, and pursuing. I've kept on hoping in spite of my many miscarriages and lost dreams. I've kept on holding on to my purpose and destiny. Don't let go of your purpose and destiny, stand and fight for it!

Chapter 20
My Surrender

I remember it just as clearly as it was yesterday. I was in a mid-week Wednesday night service in the balcony of Sweetwater Church of the Valley with the church youth group and I was only there because of a cute girl. Jennifer Walla was her name. Praise God for cute girls who invited young men like me to church services.

I was in the service and that Pastor preached a beautiful message with a salvation call at the end of the service. He began to call on people to come forward to the altar who needed salvation and they began to come. I was sitting up in the balcony because the church was packed that night; it was during what I would call the glory days of that particular church. I was sitting up there and I remember thinking to myself that I couldn't wait for that service to be over so I could keep putting the moves on this young lady I was with, and that fiery Pastor wouldn't end the service that night he just kept right on going and going. He actually held the service up for some strange reason. He said, "The Lord shows me that there is one more young person that needs to come down to this altar tonight and I'm going to hold up the service just for them. I'm going to wait for that person if it takes all night because God has a special plan for this young man." For some strange reason, I just knew that one young man was me.

He began to ask that person to raise their hand so he could see them and invite them to come to the altar as the others did. I began to sit on my hands so one of them wouldn't go up. I am telling you that I literally sat on my hands, and the girl I was there for started to put her head down and began to close her eyes very tight and started to pray hard for me. She'd only stop long enough to look at me with one eye open to see if I had responded by lifting up my hand and then when she could see I hadn't, she would again put her head down, close her eyes even tighter and she'd pray harder. I think she looked at me a couple of times and everything in her wanted to ask me, "Do you want me to go up there with you?" but she didn't. She'd just look at me as if she was saying, "you know you need to go forward now raise your hand dummy!" I just know she was saying in her heart, "Lord, get him, Lord, save him. I can't date him unless he's saved!" I couldn't go anywhere with her without her parents knowing who, what, where, when, and how close I was to her. In fact, my first date with her was to meet her parents, and I'm telling you they drilled me, ministered to me for an hour and a half in the front room of their house, and tried to lead me to Christ almost every night I came to visit and spend time with her.

I continued to sit on my hands, when all of a sudden the Preacher said, "I know who you are and you're in the balcony." Boy, did I start sweating. That man was a prophet; he knew exactly who I was. He was a seer; God reveals things to His prophets. I sat on my hands and all I can say is that I just felt the Holy Spirit pulling them up, and I couldn't do anything about it. Finally, my right hand raised and he said, "Thank you, thank you young man. I knew it was you and I was about ready to call you out if you didn't raise your hands soon." From that day forward, the divine Seed of heaven, Jesus Christ impregnated the spiritual womb of my life, and from that day forward I have never been the same. My destiny was birthed through a prophetic Pastor named Glenn Foster who told me that I had a purpose and a destiny and that I would become someone that God wanted to use for His purposes in the Kingdom of God. I just want to take this time to say Thank you Jesus, and thank you Pastor Foster, and thank you Jennifer, for seeing what I could not see in myself.

I have been on a long journey of knowing and serving Him. My mother would say, "He's been on very long journey and I went every step of the way with that boy." My mother Racheal was like my Mary and I was kind of like her Jesus. She knew from my birth that the Lord had a special call on my life, a divine purpose and destiny to follow. She knew it would lead me to many places but she followed me wherever the Lord led me in His plan and purpose for my life, through all the good, the bad and ugly places of my development. That wasn't an "Oh he's a momma's boy thing," it was a Godly healthy thing. She thanked God the day I was saved because I was like hell on earth for her and my father before that. Believe me, I gave them many gray hairs upon their head. My mother just prayed, and prayed. How many know your mom or your dad can pray, but only you can make the choice to serve God and change? My mom helped to create the spiritual womb; she created the environment; she put me in a Christian school so I would have the Godly influence in my life and God used it and that special girl Jennifer that set the hook in my mouth. From that day forward, I was never the same. A spiritual seed impregnated me. The prophecy that night was that I would be doing what I'm doing today; traveling the nations of the world ministering the gospel of Jesus Christ.

Just over the last couple of years there has been prophecies being fulfilled in my life that were given to me at age 16. That's how long they were released over my life, but sometimes that's how long you have to be pregnant with purpose and destiny before birthing comes. Are you willing to wait? It's true of the saying 'great things come to those who wait.' Just surrender to the Spirit of God and you too will give birth to your life's true purpose and destiny.

Chapter 21
Miscarriages and Lost Dreams

How many have miscarried in the natural? Maybe you started having the symptoms and changes started coming. You realized that you were indeed pregnant, but then you miscarried. How many of you know that this can be a lost dream? Some of you have been impregnated in your spiritual life. You were on fire when you first came to the Lord. You were impregnated with a passion to do something for God and then over a period of time, and after a course of events, you miscarried spiritually and so you have some lost dreams, disappoints and hurts. Maybe you've been in ministry and God's done some great things in and through you. Maybe some wonderful things have transpired and things have come alive and possibly even been birthed through your influence in ministry. Somewhere along the way, however, you got hurt and you miscarried. Now you're walking in that hurt, disappointment, and lack of forgiveness and it has knocked you out of the race and you've lost your vision and your dreams.

There is a difficult and unfortunate scenario in pregnancy called miscarriage. You start out well; life begins to form on the inside of you, but then something goes wrong and then a miscarriage occurs. You quit dreaming, you quit believing that you could ever become pregnant again, and you opt for a survival strategy and a maintenance mentality; just trying to make it from day to day. It's very much like a young woman who so desires to get pregnant and begins to see the evidence, but for some reason she suffers the unfortunate event of miscarriage and then she can become discouraged. She begins to view herself as a woman who is not complete.

Many people have miscarried and they give up the dream and they stop believing altogether. Something like this can create spiritual endometriosis in their heart just like some women in the natural suffer with endometriosis, it prevents pregnancy. They try to see that dream become a reality and because of the scar tissue it prevents the dream from taking place. It prevents the birthing, the pushing, and it prevents the purpose, and the plan. How many know there is life after miscarriage and there is definitely life after endometriosis. I'm going to release this portion of the book to my beautiful wife, Phaedra. She's going to share her testimony about miscarriages and lost dreams in hopes that it will bring hope, healing, and purpose back into your life again. Please hear what the Lord is saying through her:

I've never shared my testimony like this before, but I know this is the timing of the Lord. In general, I am a pretty private person, so God really had to speak to me to share. In my prayer time I've been asking the Lord to use me in whatever way He sees fit; I just want to be a willing vessel. Who are we to tell the Lord no anyway? I never have been pregnant or miscarried, so I can't share on that aspect, but my life has been a really long road from the beginning of our marriage. My husband and I got married in February 14, 1997 and I became a mom that day. I have a beautiful son named Brian James; he was 7 years old on our wedding day. I not only married my husband that day, but I also married my son. He was in our wedding, and I made a covenant and a commitment to him, to love him, and to be his mom. I love him with all my heart; I couldn't imagine what it would be like without him in my life. I couldn't imagine having a natural child and loving that child any more than I love my son, Brian. I just can't comprehend how it would be any different. He is my son; God blessed me with him. One time, a couple of weeks after we got married I called Brian my stepson, and that is the only time I have ever said that again. I immediately felt everything in me go, 'yuck'! I couldn't even say the words, because he's not my stepson; he is MY son. I made a vow to love him and to raise him as my own natural son and I intend on keeping that vow until my final breath.

Before we got married, we had talked about waiting a few years to have another child so we could focus on being the "three of us" for a while. Right after we got married, however, my husband and I went on our honeymoon and we began talking about getting pregnant sooner because B.J. was already 7 years old. We thought it might be better to get pregnant right away so that B.J. could have a brother or sister and they would be closer in age. We didn't want to wait after all. We started trying to get pregnant right away and began hoping and praying. We waited on the Lord and nothing happened. Months, and months, went by. By now, we were probably nearing a year and still nothing was happening so we thought maybe we should go to the doctor to see what we could do. So, off we went to the doctor together and we shared with him that we wanted to get pregnant, but nothing was happening.

He wanted to wait about a year and a half before he started any testing, so he sent us home and told us to just keep trying for a few more months. His reasons were because we were newlyweds and we already have a son which is a lot of stress in itself. Well, we had started our church ministry in July of the same year. So, not only were we newlyweds, but we had started a brand new church, I was a brand new mom and there was really a lot happening all at once. The doctor said he felt, considering the circumstances, it was a lot to take in and he really felt we should wait to do the testing. Of course, I didn't want to hear that news because we were so anxious. I was looking forward to getting pregnant.

Well, a year and a half went by, and still nothing. We went to the doctor and started some testing. All the tests we had done were coming back great. The doctor said everything was fine and, so far, he could see no complications. All the blood work was great, and the exams were great. Then we went in to do an ultrasound and that's when they found the endometriosis. We didn't know what that was so we began doing research on it to educate ourselves on what it was. Endometriosis is on the lining of the uterus (forgive me if this gets to personal for some of you) and it had produced scar tissue around the uterus. It had gone throughout my abdomen. There is no cure for endometriosis. It's hereditary and it can prevent pregnancy if left untreated. That was our first discouraging word. The doctor didn't think it was that bad because I was young at the time, only 27. He suggested we could do laparoscopic outpatient surgery that would remove a lot of the scar tissue and hopefully then I would become pregnant. He said these were our options: surgery or keep trying. We decided to try surgery and put some of our hope in that procedure.

The first year and a half of this whole process was not that big of a deal. We weren't overly discouraged; we just kept hoping and praying at that point. We did the surgery and thought we would get pregnant right after, and of course, nothing happened. We went through this for five years; this was a difficult and discouraging five-year process for me. Finally, we decided to start checking into fertility specialists. When you go there the first thing they do is re-do all the testing you previously had. They tested everything on both of us. Other than endometriosis, everything came back great. No problems; they could see no reason why we weren't getting pregnant. They do extensive testing at the fertility doctor. It's different than your primary care doctor, but even all those new tests came back fine. They said there is no reason why I should be having problems after the surgery I've had, everything looks cleared up.

All throughout this lengthy process everyone knew we were trying to get pregnant because we were excited, so we told everyone. We opened our big mouths and now it became overwhelming because everyone was in our business. Every month people keep asking, "Are you pregnant? Are you pregnant?" We really wished we never said anything at all. I know people mean well, but when you're in such a discouraging place, it's really the last thing you want to hear.

I remember my favorite part was when everyone wanted to give me "good" advice: Just relax, Take a vacation. One couple told us to drink a glass of red wine every night before bed. Everyone had their own piece of advice, and their own remedy for us. "Just keep praying." "Relax....", "Don't stress out." I felt that none of this really had anything to do with it. I know everyone meant well, but it was a lot being tossed at us, and a lot to go through. I think because we were senior pastors trying to get pregnant, so many visiting ministries would hear that we were wanting more children, and therefore had a prophetic word for me every time. I can't even count the prophetic words I've had spoken over me: "You're going to get pregnant; you're going to be a mom, by this date you're going to get pregnant." I began to put my hope in that; after all, why would a prophet just come in and say something like that? Then when it wouldn't come to pass as I had hoped I would get so upset, I would be become discouraged, I would cry, I was a wreck at times; I felt like I was on an emotional roller coaster.

We decided to try In-vitro fertilization. We spent thousands of dollars, and I had to get daily injections of fertility meds, which were very expensive. We drove down to Mexico to buy the injections so we could afford them. We really had no choice because in the States these shots were $1,200.00 for a month supply. No insurance companies would pay for it. So we would drive all the way down to Mexico because the same exact drugs were only $300.00 there. We had to scrimp and save for these procedures. One of my best friends Tiffany had given us $600.00 for one of the in-vitro fertilizations. She has known me for so many years, and she just knew my heart, and knew my desire, so she took money out of her own savings account and gave it to us as a gift. She had no expectations of getting it back (Thank you Tiff).

When we went to the doctor's office for ultrasounds, they told us the first In-vitro that we did I had 12 eggs, so the Dr. did the insemination. Well, wouldn't you know, being excited as we were, we opened our big mouths again, and we told everyone I had 12 eggs and we just know that we are going to get pregnant! The day came when we realized we were not pregnant and I was a mess. It was so emotionally draining. I praised the Lord that I didn't go into depression. I can't even tell you how horrible that feels to be in that position. If you weren't a strong person in the Lord, or didn't have the Lord – which I can't even imagine going through this without Him, because it is an emotional roller coaster. It can be devastating. After the second time of trying in-vitro, I told my husband I just couldn't go through this again. If I would have done it again where I was emotionally at the time, I probably would have just given up and possibly even walked away from the Lord in bitterness. It's so hard to be in that place and be so devastated. Your dream, whatever it may be, and for men, thinking about your dream, you thought it was going to happen this way or expected it to happen that way and it doesn't. But God knows better; He has a better plan and a purpose.

We put all our hope in these prophesies because it was the only hope we had left. When you want something so bad and someone says to you, "thus saith the Lord, "I see you pregnant…" You hang on to it because it gives you a sense of hope. You see, ever since I was a little girl I dreamed of being pregnant. So their "words" brought such hope to me, I held onto every promised word. My husband walked through it with me so wonderfully and I had his support all the way through; praise God for supportive husbands!

In the midst of all this going on, we went to minister at Sweetwater Church of the Valley. I'm the quiet one in the family; as I said, this is all new to me. I'm not a speaker; I am totally a background kind of person. I am fine with that, in fact, I'm great with it. As we were sitting there listening to the word, the Pastor speaking that night called my husband and I up to the altar to help him minister. He also called up a couple of other leadership couples too. He asked all of us to stand up on the altar beside our spouses. Then this evangelist from out of town began calling couples out. He didn't know us and we didn't know him, but he must have somehow known that we were Senior Pastors. He said to the rather large congregation that night if you had female issues, like endometriosis, or infertility come over to this couple right here, (speaking about us), and get in a line in front of them. I'm thinking in my mind – "oh my gosh!" What is this man talking about?' I have to be honest I didn't handle it very well because I was in a place of discouragement; I just wanted to run out of there. Such a huge hope and dream in my life had not happened and I was becoming more and more discouraged about it. To had to stand up there and smile, put on a happy face, and minister to other people, when I just wanted to burst out crying.

Now you have to understand that this is during a time when all my girlfriends are getting pregnant; all of them all at once, or so it seemed. The wave came in threes. I got to the point that when they would call, with a fake happy voice I would say, "Oh, that's so great. I'm so happy for you." I'd get off the phone with them and just break down and cry. I wanted to be happy for them, but I just couldn't because I was just so upset. I said, "Lord, I have given my whole life for You. I'm serving You, I'm working for You, why do I have to go through all this?" I was kicking and screaming in the beginning. I was a baby, who was pouting and kicking my feet. I felt this wasn't right or fair. I was feeling like I shouldn't have to go through this. "I gave my life for you, God!" I just felt that I was living my life for Him, and here are all these heathens not living for God much less serving Him who were getting pregnant. I said, "What's the deal? They're not even living for you Lord!" I remember getting so mad and thinking to myself, I want a baby. Believe me, it was not a pretty sight! Then I would hear about someone who was going to have an abortion and I would get so mad. I would end up getting mad at God. I would say, "God, I want a baby so bad and these people are just throwing them away. They have no regard for human life and there are so many people out there who want babies so badly – like me!" But thank God for His grace that kept me through all this.

Getting back to the Sweetwater Church story, this minister had called out endometriosis. Well, at this point we had walked through this for 5 years! I was at my lowest. I didn't even want to go that night, but friends had encouraged me to go; "Come on, it'll be good." So we went and he ends up calling us up there, which those who know me, know I don't like that kind of attention anyway. So here I am up there and now he says, "If you have had female issues, endometriosis, or infertility come over to this couple right here." All these girls got in my line saying they had endometriosis and they can't get pregnant. I was saying to myself, "Okay God, why on earth are you having me pray for these people; I'm mad, I'm totally being a baby, I'm bitter, I don't want to pray for these ladies." I was so bad! I was grumbling and complaining the whole time. I had to be obedient, since I couldn't run out of the church. Finally, by the end of the night, I was weeping with all these women. As I thought about it, and started praying for them and all their hurts and needs, I realized God had to have them come to my line because I knew exactly what they were going through. The things that they were saying I could pray so specifically for. I knew what all the terms meant, and all the emotions they were feeling. If they had gone up to anyone else, they may not have been as effective in their prayer over them as I was. I know God had me walk through all of this for a purpose and specific a reason.

It took me a long time to get to the other side. I did not walk through all of this easily. Most of the time, I didn't walk through it gracefully; it was not pretty at times. I thought to myself, "If I had to go to just one more baby shower I was not going to handle it well." I was so miserable inside myself. It was not a good place to be. The Holy Spirit finally walked me through it. I am so thankful that I kept my trust in God and did not turn away from the Lord. There were times where I had thought, "What is the point? If giving my life to You means this, what's the point?" This was where I was in my thinking; "I'm giving my all for You; why can't You just do this one thing for me?" I didn't get it; I didn't understand it. It took me a few years of going around the mountain until I got to the point where I could honestly rejoice for my friends and church members when they got pregnant. Brian and I became more, and more, quiet about what we were going through. We just focused on the Lord and did not share much if anything about our personal lives in this area. We did not communicate with anybody.

It took me a long time to get to the point of being happy for people, and not being angry or putting the blame on God. I finally had to get to the point where I gave up on my dream of being pregnant. I said, "Lord, You must have a better plan for my life." I thought I knew how it was going to turn out. I thought I knew what God was going to do in my life. I just thought I knew how everything was going to transpire and when it didn't happen the way I wanted it to, I threw a fit. I fully surrendered to God and said, "God, You know my heart, You know I want a baby; but I give up and I trust You. I trust that Your plans are better for my life."

People closest to us knew what we had gone through and they started saying "what about adoption?" The thought of adoption just made me really mad. "Why do I have to adopt?" I thought to myself. I had a really terrible attitude about it. I kept thinking, "Why can't God just do this for me? Why do I have to adopt?"

I realized that you have to come to a place where you surrender all and say, "God You have a purpose for my life and I don't know how to do things but You do." Even though you think you know what's best for you, you can't see the future and know what God has in store for you. I want to share what God did in my life once I finally surrendered to His purpose and plan for my life.

I finally got over my horrible attitude about adoption. It wasn't that I felt badly about adoption, I was just mad that my dream didn't happen my way. I just didn't know why I had to do it this way and go through the process. Brian and I finally decided that we either remained the three of us forever, which would have been fine, or we pursue the possibility of adoption. I knew in my heart that I had to do something so we decided to adopt which is another whole emotional process in itself.

I don't know if you have ever known anyone who's adopted, but the process takes a minimum of a year and it is so in depth. You're given personality tests, home inspections, and your whole life history from the time you were born. They want to know your relationship with your parents, your siblings, your grandparents, if you were ever abused. Everything you could ever imagine; they're in your business. It's a very, very long process and there were times where my husband and I asked ourselves, is all of this really worth it. It's hard to get certified to adopt. We just knew in our hearts that we were to continue and do this. We went through the Christian Family Care Agency in Phoenix, AZ. We were blessed to have great caseworkers. We had to go through eight weeks of parenting classes, adoption classes, and fertility classes. They had to ask me all these questions to determine if I was harboring any bitterness, or resentment about being infertile, or if I had anger in my heart. We weathered the storm with the Lord, and made it through, and we finally got our certification in January of 2002.

Now, when we filled out our adoption paperwork my husband and I had talked everything out, and we felt we would just help God along because we knew exactly what we wanted. We just want one more child, a girl, and it will be done, that's it, simple, right? We only signed up for a girl. With an adoption you can be very specific. You can sign up for anything you want like a boy or girl, hair color, skin color, nationality, how old or how young, whatever. By doing this, you may be on the waiting list for years, but you can be that specific. We weren't that specific; we said we wanted a girl, white or Hispanic, under 12 months old. We didn't sign up for a boy. We never signed up for a boy because we already had a boy so we only wanted a girl, we only wanted two children.

One day I was driving to Wal-Mart and I bought this little fish, I don't know why; just out of the blue I bought a fish and took him home. I don't know if it was a boy, I just kept saying 'him.' I took him home and showed him to my husband. He then said to me; "Babe, you bought a fish?" This was not like me, so I think he was trying to figure this out in his mind. I started asking him what we should name him. At this point, he's just looking like he doesn't know, he doesn't care… whatever. But I finally drew him in with this cute little beta fish. We went through all these different names together. Nothing came to mind we could agree on, so we stopped trying that evening.

The next morning I got up for work and got in my car. At the time, we had a two door car and on my drive in I started praying about a car. "Lord, we need a four door car, and I want it to be purple. I love purple." I was being very specific. I knew it would be so difficult to crawl through to the back of a two-door car for a child's car seat. I just knew that God was going to bless us. Here I am praying and telling the Lord I really need this purple, four-door car. Just as I was praying, I started thinking about my fish. I just decided, all of a sudden, to name this fish Mike. I don't know why, but it just came to me out of the blue. I named him Mike. When I got to work, I told my husband the Lord had given me the fish's name. He looks at me like OK..., he asked, "Well? What is it?" I said, "Mike." He says, "Mike? What is that? Why on earth would you name a fish Mike? I was thinking you were going to name it Jonah or flipper or something like that." "No..." I said, "I don't know why, but his name is Mike."

That afternoon while we were at the church working the phone rang. It was our caseworker. She says, "Hi, we have this little boy, he needs a home," and she told me a couple of things about him, but the whole time she's talking, I'm not hearing what she's saying, all I'm hearing and all I'm stuck on is that it's a boy. I didn't sign up for a boy. I don't want two boys, we already have a boy we want a daughter. I didn't hear much of what she said after that. I just couldn't get past it. I just kept thinking; "we didn't even check the boy box on our application." I'm thinking, "Lady, why are you even calling me? Did you misunderstand the girl check mark?" I decided to just humor her and at the end of the phone conversation I asked, "Well, what's his name?" She said, "Oh, I don't know, I forgot to ask." So I said to her, "Alright, well when you find out his name let me know." I don't even know what made me ask that. I told her I would talk to Brian and call her back later. She said to let her know, because if not, they needed to find a new home for this little boy. When I got off the phone with her, I said, "It's a boy, Brian, why are they even calling us? We didn't sign up for a boy."

Next I called my mom, "Okay mom. There calling me about this boy and I don't even want another boy. I don't want two boys!" She had this sneaky little giggle and I was thinking, what is that about. She said, "Well, I didn't want to tell you this before, but the Lord gave me a vision of a boy. I just saw this little boy; I saw his face and everything." Now I'm thinking, "Oh, brother, this is just great!"

Next I called my mother-in-law. "Mom, they just called me and they have this boy." She asked me what his name was and I told her we didn't know his name. She says, "Boy, that's weird, wouldn't you think that's one of the first things someone would ask? What's his name?" Then she says out of the blue, "Well, I woke up this morning and I kept hearing the name "Mike." She said she didn't know who it was, but she just started praying for a Mike. I told her that this was weird because I had just named my fish Mike that same morning. Then Brian's mom said that she started singing that old song, "My name is Michael. I've got a nickel." You know that old song. She's singing that song on the way to work. Well, we thought this was all very strange, and went on with our day.

A couple hours later my caseworker calls me back and she says, "The foster mom just called me, his name is Michael. (I almost dropped the phone!) Then I knew it, so I said. "Okay God, I give up; we'll take him, and give him a good home." There was no denying it, we had three confirmations: first, why would I name a fish Mike? How weird is that? Second; then there's my mom. She had never told me about what she had seen because she knew my hope was for a girl. Third, I call my mother-in-law and she's singing a song about Michael on her way to work. So I said, "Okay God, I can't even argue with You." That's how we got our sweet son, Michael.

It's totally, God ordained for this boy to be in our family. Nobody could tell me differently. He looks just like my husband. He was almost three years old when he came to live with us. We were his seventh home. This precious boy had gone from home, to home. The last home he was in was a very strong Mormon family. He was one of nine children. He could barely talk, and he wasn't potty trained. He was so far behind with all these other children. He didn't even have to talk with so many kids in this family, they just spoke for him. God brought him out of that Mormon home. Not that it was a bad home, but God had a plan to move him out of there and into our home.

While all of this was going on, we had just purchased a new church building for our congregation and we were in the process of adopting this group of people into our church family who needed new spiritual parents a new church family. This all happened in December 2001 and then on February 16, 2002 Michael came to live with us forever. We walked through a spiritual adoption of a congregation and a natural adoption with Michael at the same time. When Michael was new to our home we had only brought him to church the second or third time when we had a mighty prophet of the Lord at the church and he started prophesying over Michael. He gave him this incredible prophesy that he was going to be a prophet to the nations. He said he was given to us by the Lord for me and my husband to raise and train up in the prophetic, he's our little prophet. We speak that over him all the time.

Well, everything is going great and in the midst of all this we're still keeping things open in our own life for the possibility of pregnancy. We just felt if it happens, it happens. We still hoped and prayed. We thought maybe God wanted us to adopt this boy and now He would allow me to get pregnant, but without going into a lot of detail, I ended up having to get a total hysterectomy done in March of 2003.

As I said in the beginning, there is no cure for endometriosis. Once you have surgery, from what the doctors have told me, it comes back twice as bad as before. Basically, you're clearing out all the scar tissue, but the disease doesn't go away, and it just comes back to do more damage. They told me it was so bad that there was really no more hope.

My doctor didn't want to rush right in and do a hysterectomy because I was still so young and didn't have any natural kids even though I had two boys. She still was leery of doing it. We wanted to wait about six months and pray about it. My mom had just passed away of uterine cancer, and the kind she had was hereditary and with the endometriosis my doctor just thought we should get rid of everything. She wanted to give me time to really think about it and not jump into anything.

We really sought the Lord and I truly had a great peace about it like I've never had before. I knew it was the right decision for me. I had to die to the dream of being pregnant; I would never, ever become pregnant. I really prayed about it and put a lot of thought into it. You know, God promised me I would be a mom, but He never promised me I would be pregnant. He did promise me I would have children, but He didn't tell me how. I had to die to that. Once I got to that point, and once His peace had come to my heart about this, I had the surgery.

The endometriosis was so bad. The surgery was only supposed to take an hour and I was in surgery for three and a half hours. It was so complicated that my Dr. had to call in two specialists. All the scar tissue had wrapped around my appendix. If she had not taken it out when she did, it would have ended up rupturing. All the scar tissue was just squeezing the appendix. It was certain there was no hope of a pregnancy; I had to get to a peaceful understanding and acceptance of this. I went through a grieving process, because it was like a death.

Before we went into the surgery, we had called the case worker and told her we wanted to adopt a little girl now. We had adopted Michael and he had been in our home almost a year and he was adjusting so well. He was growing by leaps and bounds. His speech was doing so much better, so we felt now would be a good time to adopt again. We had never cut off our certification because we knew we wanted to have a little girl eventually. This time I told her "Please; please do not call me for a little boy. I definitely do not want three boys. Don't even call me for a boy." We were joking around about it. She told me we could be on the list for a year or more because we wanted a little girl about a year old. She explained to us again that with our choices being so specific it could take up to a year possibly longer. We told her that was fine; it will be in the timing of the Lord. We weren't worried about it. I told her we were not in any rush.

I went in for my surgery on my birthday, March 4, 2003. While I was in the hospital, my husband received a phone call from the case worker that they had a little girl. Here they had just told me at the end of February it could be a year or more, and it had only been two weeks. When she said that, we just said, "Okay, well we know God's timings is different than man's timing."

March 24th, 2003, Twenty days after they removed all of my reproductive organs, we were blessed with our daughter. The daughter I dreamed about all those years came home to live with us forever. We named her Abigail Rose. She was four months old, and she was a total miracle of the Lord. God is so good! She was abandoned in the hospital by her birth mother who was addicted to cocaine. She came out of the womb a cocaine addicted baby. But God is so good because she has never shown any signs of addiction withdrawal or any other problems the cocaine could have caused in life.

> After I had healed from my surgery we went back to church with our new baby, and everybody teased with me saying they had never met a woman who went into the hospital to have a full hysterectomy and came out with a newborn baby girl. God is so good, and we are just so thankful. You see, if I didn't surrender to the Lord, and trust Him, I would not have my three beautiful children. We truly believe the God took Michael and Abbi out of a potentially harmful lifestyle and placed them in our care to be raised up and trained up for the Lord.
>
> I want to thank you for allowing me to share my testimony. I want to tell you that, yes, it was so hard for me to go through all that, but to come out on the other side victorious is awesome! I just want to be an encouragement to women who are going through the same things that I have gone through. God has a plan and He can use anything. No matter what you have gone through, I want to encourage you to share your testimony with others. God will use those things to touch and change hearts and lives and bring them into their divine purpose and destiny and His plan for their life, even if the thing you felt that you have walked through is small, He can still use those things too. Be willing and obedient to Him and He will use it heal others in the same position you were in.
>
> Blessings, Pastor Phaedra Alton

I want to say a sincere thank you to my wife for sharing her testimony with you. As you can see, she has walked through some pretty difficult things in her life even while pursuing her own purpose and destiny. I know it was difficult for her to share and expose such intimate details of her life but I know that it has touched, and possibly transformed someone's life today.

I want the Lord to plant these seeds inside of you. The Lord never said it would be easy to follow Him, in fact, Jesus said in Matthew 10:39, "He who finds his life will lose it, and he who loses his life for My sake will find it." When it seemed as if my wife was losing everything she held dear in her life, in God's purposes (not her own) she found her life again. I went through all of these things along side of her, but of course, it was much worse for her as it seemed as if all her hopes and dreams she had desired since childhood were removed when they surgically removed her ability to give birth.

She says she walked through everything badly, but I say she did very well for all she had to go through emotionally. Don't get me wrong, she did have some pretty rough moments, but she weathered them better than anyone I know could have. I know it was hard for her to be a Pastors wife and a woman of faith and all that carries with it when she felt as if everything was crashing down around her emotionally. She doesn't like to be fake, and she is certainly not a pretender. There were days when it was all she could do just to function and be a good mother to our son B.J. and good wife to myself. I could see the Lord loving her and preparing her through every phase of this wonderful testimony. God was doing incredible little mini-miracles all along the way throughout this five-year process in the Spirit.

My wife mentioned in her story that we had just bought a church building, we used to call it 'the purple church' because everything - and I mean everything - in it was royal purple. When we bought the building we weren't just buying a building made by man, we were spiritually adopting a people that were not our own. The Lord was teaching and preparing us in the spiritual realm how to become adoptive parents in the natural. The Lord has such a wonderful sense of humor. You see, God said, "I'm going to take two churches that don't know each other at all, from two entirely different church cultures and backgrounds, and put them together and make them one family!"

There was just a small remnant of people who were left attending the previous church that we had bought; making a long spiritual adoptive story short; many good things transpired in this unification process. There was a small, yet strong, remnant group that remained and joined up with our church. The people had to learn to love us; we had to learn to love them. They had to learn to receive and appreciate our backgrounds and church culture; we had to learn to receive and appreciate them and their backgrounds. But praise God now we are one big, happy family. Because of the spirit of adoption working in our midst, we don't see each other as two separate churches any longer but one family in Christ. I'm not saying there haven't been some issues, and some troubles along the way in this journey either. There are difficult moments in all families. Blended families especially have to learn to love each other and work with each other. Ultimately, we were what they needed; they needed good spiritual parents because things that had transpired in their ministry had caused them to lose hope in leaders; many of them were really wounded. So when we came in, we went beyond the call of duty to win their hearts; to show them what good spiritual parents we were willing to be. We made sure to show them they could put their trust in us, and in like manner, they embraced us.

Some of those folks that joined our family are the most loyal and hardest working servants we have in our church. We are one in the body of Christ. God did some great things in us back then. He taught us in the spiritual realm that prepared us for what He was about to do in the natural realm. It was amazing, because after we learned how to receive and love a group of people that were not our own, the Lord lead us into doing the very same as natural adoptive parents in a practical way for both Michael and Abigail.

As you heard in Phaedra's testimony about Michael, even though he is not my blood son, he really looks so much like me. Of course the funny joke people enjoy using on me is, "Pastor, where were you on the day Michael was conceived? And who were you with?" He looks like a little mini-me, and the age he was when we first got him fit perfectly with how long Phaedra and I were married so no one has questioned his belonging.

Let me also say that it has always been my dream to have a baby girl. I wanted a little Hispanic girl because I myself am half Mexican, and it was always my mother's dream to have a Hispanic granddaughter running around to spoil and to teach her about our culture. God knows how to work it all together and orchestrate it, doesn't He? It wasn't just Phaedra's dream to have a baby girl; the Lord met my dream, He met my mother's, and the Lord met our son Brian's dream to have siblings running around.

Throughout this difficult journey I prophesied to my wife a lot; I'm sure that at times I probably made it much harder on her because I felt a responsibility to help her keep the dream alive and to keep her faith alive. I must say that in some extreme and intense moments it was like giving her C.P.F.R. That stands for Cardio Pulmonary Faith Resuscitation. I felt that was my job as her husband and as the priest (the spiritual leader) of our home. I would say to her softly, and yet prophesying with all confidence and boldness of spirit "Honey, God's not done with what He told us He would do." I also want you to know that the prophets that came to our church to minister came from all over the country and around the world, and most of them didn't know a thing about what was happening in our lives when they came and spoke into our lives about God's plan for children. In fact, one of them came in and prophesied we'd have a little boy and a little girl not far apart in age. Michael and Abbi are only four years apart. Then a great man of God by the name of Kelly Varner prophesied that we'd be sipping on iced tea in our backyard watching the children God gave to us play together. It wasn't long after when the Lord reminded us that this happened when we were sitting in our backyard on a new patio set we had bought and we were watching all three of our children play together in the backyard. Those prophetic words were God's way of speaking to us and telling us that He had a plan all along to fulfill our purpose and destiny.

We have our mindsets, and our own pre-conceived ideas, on how we think God's going to do what He's going to do in our lives. He's the only One who knows the plan, Phaedra said it right. We dissected and reviewed every one of those prophecies and every one of them said you will have children, not that you will become pregnant. There is only one prophecy that said she would be pregnant, but it described the spiritual and emotional pregnancy that she would have to walk through to be able to bring these children into our home. Again, the Lord promised we would have children, but He didn't tell us how they would get there. He physically brought them to our doorstep with one phone call. The same thing can happen in your life. What have you believed God for? What's this thing that He placed on the inside of you? It may not be exactly how you think it's going to happen. It's all about God's promise. His promises have all superseded everything that I have ever hoped or dreamed for, and it can and will happen in your life as well.

> "Eye has not seen, nor ear heard, Nor have entered into the heart of man The things which God has prepared for those who love Him. But God has revealed them to us through His Spirit. For the Spirit searches all things, yes, the deep things of God." (I Corinthians 2:9-10)

The key is to not allow yourself to get spiritual endometriosis. That can happen to anyone no matter who they are or how spiritual they are. It doesn't matter how strong you think you are; how gifted you are; how knowledgeable of the Word you are; or how much you love Jesus. You can still get spiritual endometriosis that will cause you to become bitter, numb, and infertile to the plans and purposes of God in your life. Yes, my wife had physical endometriosis, but she allowed herself for a season to get spiritual endometriosis as well. All those disappointments, lost dreams, and miscarriages will create spiritual endometriosis in our life. When she finally died to the dream, and she lost her life, she found it. That's why we both say and preach with conviction that God doesn't waste anything in your life. He uses everything; your hurts, your pains, and yes, even your disappointments. He uses those things to bring you love, joy, happiness, prosperity, goodness, and God's divine plan and purpose for your life. He will turn all those things around for your good.

> "We know that in all things God works for the good of those who love him. He appointed them to be saved in keeping with His purpose."
>
> Romans 8:28

Although we were going through all those difficult things together just to have children, we still had to be the man and woman of faith for the ministry God gave us to serve Him in. So there are going to be times where it seems fake, produced, or made up, but keep on doing what you know is right. Keep on praying, confessing, hoping, and dreaming. Keep prophesying, and declaring it! I kept telling her, "Honey, it's going to happen. The prophets declared it and the Bible tells me if we receive a prophet then we shall receive a prophet's reward. Honey, you and I deserve that reward!"

> "He that receives a prophet in the name of a prophet shall receive a prophet's reward." (Matthew 10:41)

I reminded Phaedra that there's an apostolic and prophetic anointing on our ministry and what the enemy is trying to do is get us distracted and disillusioned with prophecy. It didn't really affect me as much because I knew that when someone prophesies over you today, it could happen ten years down the road. Here she was getting these prophecies and visions: everybody had a vision, a word, and a prophecy for her. In most every case, it was truly honest and sincere as people desire to encourage you in faith, but if you do come from that kind of church culture, it's important that you listen to the Lord, and not everybody else. You heard her say this more than once in her testimony; we learned not to open our mouths. Sometimes you just need to be quiet and leave it in the hands of the Lord. You learn about yourself, and about whom you are, and then you learn who He is in you. There is a family picture in my office that has captured our testimony. It is so incredible how my son, B.J. looks so much like Phaedra even though she was not his birth mother, and the other two look so much like me and my mother. When we are all together it looks very natural, like we have been together forever. We may have not known for a while what God was doing, but God knew exactly what He was doing. Trust in Him!

Chapter 22
Are You Birthing an Isaac or an Ishmael?

How we see ourselves in relation to God, will orchestrate all that we are and all that we do in this world. We live in a success driven world so it's important that we view our failures through the eyes of God. This is absolutely to our success in living a life of purpose and destiny. God is love and the nature of that love must be the driving force behind everything we do or attempt to do for Him.

It's important we understand that a person's failures doesn't necessarily mean they are a failure. Failure often times is a pathway to success. Success is not the absence of failure. Every great man or woman, who has done something great for the Lord, or in business, or in industry, inventions, or any other pursuit; many of those who have experienced great success, have all had multiple failures in their lives before their success was achieved. Their success was a result of failure. They would fail and then they would go back to the drawing board and get it right.

That is what the Lord does for us; He turns our failures into success. In fact, failure has some benefits. Have you ever made a mistake? Welcome to the human race. It just means you're alive. The Bible says in James 3:2, "We all stumble in many ways." We are living proof of this verse, but everybody wants to be a success – nobody wants to be a failure. Come to think of it, I've never met anybody in life who's said, "My goal in life is to be a failure."

As a society, this puts a lot of stress on us because failure is a part of life. Yet, many people will do anything like lie, cheat, steal, or whatever they have to in order to succeed. Success is that important, and often times failure in America is considered the unpardonable sin. Failure doesn't have to be fatal because we value success so much, we tend to exaggerate the effects of failure, but failure isn't the end of the world; you won't die from it. With failure you fail, but you can pick yourself back up, brush the dirt of your knees, and keep moving forward. One of the best ways to bounce back from failure is to redefine it. Failure is not failing to reach your dreams, or not setting a goal and missing it. Failure is not falling down, but it is refusing to get back up. If at first you don't succeed, big deal! It's usually the second, third, or fourth time you actually get it right. You are never a failure unless you give up. Remember, everybody fails.

Did you know that one of God's primary tools in making you the kind of person He wants you to be is failure? He uses it in your life to mold you, shape you, and develop your character. While we rarely learn from our successes (because we typically attribute our success to our sheer natural talent), we can learn from our failures. We usually think of failure as being a negative experience, but wise people learn from failure and use it to their advantage. They learn and grow from it, and they use it as a stepping stone.

God often uses failure to educate us. Along the way, we figure out what doesn't work and eventually, we figure out what does. Psalm 119:71 says, "It is good for me that I have been afflicted, that I may learn Your statutes." A more modern translation of this passage could be; "My troubles turned out all for the best. They forced me to learn from God's textbook." God says, "Sometimes I have to use failure to get you into the Book so you'll start looking and realize that it's a textbook that I want to teach you."

When Phaedra and I were married, our first few years together were a little rough for me in the compatibility department. While we were both very much in love with each other and believed that God had put us together, we were total opposites and simply didn't agree on a lot of things. For example, when we would go to a furniture store to search for something for our new home, as soon as we walked in the door I would get mesmerized by certain items and she would do the same, but in the exact opposite direction. It was really hard to communicate about certain things and we couldn't negotiate very well either. If it hadn't been for the fact that we were both committed Christians and leaders who felt that divorce was not an option, we wouldn't have continued trying as much as we did to keep our marriage strong secure. But we said, "We're going to make this marriage work if it kills us", and it nearly did at times. Or maybe I should say that we nearly killed each other a few times, but we finally both swallowed our pride (I was probably more stubborn and prideful than her), and that turned our marriage around and set us on the right path. I look back now and think about some of the lessons I learned in those first few years together. They are lessons that have kept our love strong and true for one another. I look back and thank God for the failures that I experienced because they were learning experiences. God educated me through my failures with Phaedra.

God is not surprised when we fail. He knows it's going to happen. In fact, He expects it. Even when we fail, God doesn't stop loving us. That's called grace. God knows the frailties of our humanity. He doesn't expect us to be perfect, and more importantly, He doesn't stop loving us less when we fail. Often when we're in the middle of a failure, it's difficult to see God's hand in our life. Bouncing back from failure may not be the easiest thing you'll ever do in your life, but it's something that God wants to help you accomplish.

Big or small failure, it hasn't changed God's purpose and destiny for your life. Allow Him to teach you, motivate you, and grow you through your failures. He still has a plan for your life and a place for you in His Kingdom purposes in the earth. We all have weaknesses. We also know where we are the weakest in our lives. The Bible says in II Corinthians 12:9; "And he said unto me, My grace is sufficient for you: for my strength is made perfect in weakness. Therefore most gladly I will rather boast in my infirmities, that the power of Christ may rest upon me." It's hard to understand this, but what this passage is really saying is that God can take the greatest weakness we have in our life and turn it into our greatest strength. Jacob had a supplanting nature. It was a major weakness in his life that seemed to get him into a lot of trouble throughout his life. Where it really manifested was when he stole his brother's birthright in Genesis 25:29-32, but God took Jacob's supplanting nature and turned it around and used it for His glory. He turned it into one of the greatest gifts that Jacob had.

In the journey I have been on, there was a church I led before the one I pastor now that I had lost; and as I shared in great detail there was a son I lost before my promised son Brian James was born to me. If you'll notice, my life was just following suite because throughout the stories of the Bible there were always "something else" in the faith heroes lives before the true promise was manifested. For example; Abraham had a son named Ishmael before he had the promised son Isaac (See Genesis Chapter 16 & 17). The people group that was spawned from Ishmael's line wound up giving the Israelites a lot of problems later on down the road, and some would argue that they are still giving Israel a lot of grief today.

But the same is true of us spiritually as it relates to our purpose and destiny. A lot of times in life we will give birth to Ishmaels before we have our promised son Isaac. What I'm saying here is sometimes God allows us to give birth to an Ishmael so we can truly appreciate our Isaacs.

There was a reason why Ishmael was born. The people of God cast him out into the desert with his mother; they were left there to die, but then the angel of the Lord came and said, "I'm going to bless you." In spite of Abraham and Sarah taking matters into their own hands with Haggar, Sarah's servant to have a child, God still turned their mistakes around and used it for good in their lives. No one thought that Ishmael was good for anything other than to be thrown out into the middle of the desert, but God still had a plan and wound up blessing Ishmael. The moral of the story is this: don't despise your Ishmael, learn from it, and appreciate your Isaac when it comes. Many of us can learn from Ishmael's birth. You can't despise your preparation time, learn to love it. I hope this brings insight that will help you with the current Ishmaels you are dealing with in life.

> "But this is that which was spoken by the prophet Joel; And it shall come to pass in the last days, saith God, I will pour out of my Spirit upon all flesh: and your sons and your daughters shall prophesy, and your young men shall see visions, and your old men shall dream dreams: And on my servants and on my handmaidens I will pour out in those days of my Spirit; and they shall prophesy." (Acts 2:16-18, KJV)

Friends, what God is getting ready to do in our future is about to blow every one of us away. People will be saying, "It can't happen like this!" just like they did when Jesus came to Israel. They said, "He can't be the Messiah." The Lord is going to come, just like He did back then and He is going to blow away religious mindsets. We're going to be looking for Him to come one way and He'll come another way. When Jesus came riding into Jerusalem they shouted, "Hosanna!" They wanted an earthly and natural king to ride in on His great white horse and set up His kingdom in the natural in Jerusalem, but He came in on a lowly donkey. He wasn't setting up a natural kingdom, but a spiritual kingdom. Praise God! He wasn't going to be crowned with a crown of jewels; He was getting a crown of thorns. The religious people of that time said, "It can't happen like this! He can't be the Messiah!" and they missed Him. Don't try to figure all this out with your theology. Get free of that. Don't get so embedded in your church traditions that you miss the new things of God today! Elijah the prophet cried out, "Oh, I'm the only prophetic servant of God left in Israel." And the Lord said to him, "No you're not, Elijah. I've reserved many more in other regions and places. You're not God's only one anointed for the times. I have a Master Plan and purpose and you are a part of that plan."

> And there he (Elijah) went into a cave, and spent the night in that place; and behold, the word of the LORD came to him, and He said to him, "What are you doing here, Elijah?" So he said, "I have been very zealous for the LORD God of hosts; for the children of Israel have forsaken Your covenant, torn down Your altars, and killed Your prophets with the sword. I alone am left; Yet I have reserved seven thousand in Israel, all whose knees have not bowed to Baal, and every mouth that has not kissed him." (I Kings 19:9 & 18, KJV)

I'm exposing you to some import issues that we all have to face at some point or another, because you cannot live in a Charismatic, Pentecostal, bubble all your life. I believe that this kind of transparency about life as it relates to your purpose and destiny is going to teach you some very important things. There is so much more for you to learn , so you can deal with and address those difficult places and questions in life in the Spirit and under the anointing. It is important that you are informed and educated so you know what you are talking about as it relates to your future and destiny. Like King David of old I've been chased, I've had javelins thrown at me, I've been chased into caves, I've seen all of those disgruntled people come around me, but I've also seen those same kind of people turn into mighty men and women of God.

- We all go through dark and difficult times in life, just look at all the characters in the Bible; look at the dark times they all had to go through so they could appreciate the light. We've got to change the way we respond to God and to others! Don't be like this last generation of preachers that when someone's sin is exposed they all shout condemningly, "I knew they had sin in their lives it!" Then in their so called righteous judgments begin to tear them and their ministries down verbally to others in the community, kill them with their words, and like the Pharisees did to Jesus they look for ways to crucify them with their religious pious mindsets and attitudes.

- We're supposed to love them, and help them, serve them, and remit their sins not condemn them. If they confess their sin we're suppose to forgive their sin and help restore them from their fallen state, and bring them back to a healthy state. Instead, we cast stones, and spread rumors about them. We talk horribly about them and we become spiritually pious, rather than coming along side hurting and wounded people who really need love and prayer. We throw stones and words, and then we stab them with our spiritual knives. We need to be a part of a new generation of believers and ministers, who don't condemn and judge, but seek restoration and healing which can transform lives through Christ's love.

There are so many people that are not in the church today because of these horrible things. Their purpose and destinies are being delayed because of their discouragement. Be the one to help them be loved back into the body of Christ so they can complete their divine purpose and destiny. You can become a link that leads them back on course into their purpose and destiny in the Lord.

In my former ministry life and marriage to Alyce, because of her sickness I had to let go of the ministry and pass it on to someone else. Of course, that once thriving ministry died. I became very bitter and upset because

I had poured so much of my young life into it and I felt as if it was for nothing. I began thinking to myself, "Lord, if this is what I gave my life for since I was young, I don't want it anymore. I'll just continue to be a good Christian." Then, when my first wife Alyce died and I saw how devastating it was for my son B.J., I got so angry at the Lord and I said. "God, why, I gave my life to you, I served you with everything I had and this is how I am rewarded with trials, with sickness, and now death?!"

Those were some pretty dark times in my life. Back then, I thought I would just sit back and be a good Christian guy in a country band and sing all positive songs. You know what? The Holy Spirit chased me down in the bars. You know what they called me in the clubs because I was a former minister? Some of them knew about it and it began to spread it around, so they started calling me "Padre." I'd go to the club to play with the band and I'd hear, "Hey, Padre." Couldn't they call me cowboy or something? I mean, I had everything, the jeans, the boots, and the cowboy hat. I was trying to change everything so they wouldn't call me that anymore. Then they wanted me to sing Christian songs in the clubs, so I started singing them because I was asked to by all those drunks who would get emotional. When they were drinking, they would shout out, "Can you sing Amazing Grace there, Padre?" So I'd start in singing it in response to them. I'm telling you the Holy Spirit would start moving in the bar and they would be crying with a drink in their hand and whipping away their tears. You can run, but you cannot hide from your purpose and destiny.

Are any of you like me? You know when you allow what I call "stinking thinking" to start up and then all of a sudden the enemy, Satan comes in and starts to lie to you, and then he pulls you in deeper and deeper until you start believing the lie that God is just punishing you for something. In reality, it's just God allowing a circumstance to work on your character and integrity for your ultimate purpose and destiny.

I went to Bible school, and seminary. I had stuff deposited on the inside of me and here I was trying to run. I was agreeing with the devil that I was just going to be a good Christian guy, and focus on corporate America, be successful, and sing good, positive, country songs in the clubs. Now that was a challenge in itself; just trying to sing "positive" country songs.

There was one guy in country music who sang primarily positive songs, and that was Vince Gill. I knew a lot of his stuff and sang those songs over and over. The Lord met me one night on the road home from a show in Wickenburg, Arizona. We were playing in a club and we were supposed to open up for Willie Nelson. If anybody knows Willie, he likes to party. He was supposed to come do a few numbers and we had the opportunity to open before his act. It was our opportunity for fame!

From the story we were told, Willie decided he was going to party and got so stoned out of his mind that he couldn't make it to the concert. We must have played for an hour and a half trying to stall. They loved us for the first hour, but after that they began to pound on their tables saying "we want Willie; we want Willie"! Of course, our band was in the back freaking out, by this time, we've run out of music and we were wondering what we were going to do. Long story short, there was a little riot that happened; they started throwing beer bottles at us on the stage. The Sheriff's Department came flooding in, they had their dogs, and the sheriff's posse and they had to escort us through the back because those people really wanted to kill us.

The Lord met me on the ride home that night and it was almost as if it was His audible voice that I heard saying to me, "Brian, are you done yet?" I said, "Lord, I'm sorry what am I doing here?" That night I knew I was done running from my purpose and destiny. The Lord brought me full circle and I had to go to the band and tell them what God told me. Thankfully, they understood. They knew this already, and although they didn't want to lose me, in their hearts they knew what I was saying was true. I had to tell them that the Lord was not done with me and I can't run from Him anymore. They appreciated me being real with them about it; I think they knew deep down.

I left the group and never looked back. From that night on it was the beginning of the greatest days of my life. The Lord asked me if I was done yet and I told Him yes I was. He said, "Now are you ready for My Plan?" And I said, "Yes, Lord, I'm done doing it my way, I want your way or No way." From that day forward until today, some of the greatest days of my life have taken place. So those years of trial and tribulation are now like a faint dream to me. There's a wonderful verse in the Word of God that says He'll even make those difficult places of our lives as if they were just a bad dream, and that's what it is like for me now.

> "When the LORD brought back the captivity of Zion, We were like those who dream. Then our mouth was filled with laughter, and our tongue with singing. Then they said among the nations, "The LORD has done great things for them." The LORD has done great things for us, and we are glad." (Psalm 126:1-3)

You see, what He brought into my life is so magnificent that it overshadowed all those years of hurt, pain, rejection, anger and frustration. Praise God, the Lord never left me, and He never stopped speaking to me. He never stopped showing me how much He loved me and He kept pushing me toward His purpose and destiny for my life. It was right after these events that I started Desert Rose Community Church. We began with seven people in a little wedding chapel on Sunday mornings. From that day on, I continued to experience His freedom. I walked more and more into my life's purpose destiny. Desert Rose has far exceeded anything that I felt was a success in the first church I led because this is my Isaac. The other church was the Ishmael. Don't despise your Ishmaels because they teach you to appreciate your Isaacs.

Chapter 23
From Surviving To Thriving

I would venture to say that some of you have been in a place of wondering. You're not flowing in your full potential. You're trying to be a good Christian and you're trying to do good things. You're trying to do the right thing and be faithful in the place you find yourself right now, but it's just not where God wants you. God's trying to take you from a place where you're just surviving, to a place where you're thriving.

For some of you, you're in the place you know you're supposed to be, but you're just sitting idle. You're not really doing anything. You've backed off from doing the things that you use to do; things that you love doing and you have a heart to do. You have just fallen into survival mode due to lost dreams and miscarriages. You've fallen into a survival mentality and you say to yourself that you'll just sit quietly, be good, behave, and go about your business, but this is not what God wants you to do.

He's trying to get you from surviving to thriving. You need to come alive! I encourage you to respond and become obedient to the call. Even the smallest acts of obedience will bring forth great things, much fruit, and abundance. With these small acts of obedience, you'll see great breakthrough in your life. Men will reject you, but God will always love you. God sees you for who you are, where you're going, and where He wants you to be. Don't let the endometriosis of life kill your spiritual womb. Maybe it didn't happen the way you thought it was supposed to, but let Him show you the way. Maybe you're older, that's okay, men and women of the Bible were called at an older age and changed the course of nations. This is a season to complete what you've started. Be a workman who is not ashamed. Stay faithful; get equipped, and don't leave things where you started. Stop blaming others for your failures.

You know, in order to give birth we have to have our family around us; they need to be out there in the waiting rooms. Are you ready to have God's spiritual anesthetic come upon you? You are getting close to your birthing time. Many of you are close to having your spiritual water break. God is getting ready to break forth great things in your life. While you're waiting for your time of delivery, you need to be in the waiting room praying for other's deliveries. It doesn't matter how old you are, and it doesn't matter where you are in your life; God can use you to change the course of a nation. All it takes is one person, one willing heart, one yielded vessel to say yes to their purpose and yes to their destiny.

There's a reason why the Spirit of God is sending forth a message around the world about purpose and destiny. He's about to launch something powerful. A great revival is coming, and great transformation is coming. God is raising up a new generation of believers and ministers. People who are hungry, thirsty, and desperate to see the manifested presence of God! God's raising up a new breed and a Joshua generation. God has a new generation that will not be fine with wilderness warfare all of their life. They will not be fine with repeatedly going around the mountain and being fed by quail and manna. These people are strong and want the Promise Land. They want everything that God has for them. I want you to really reach out and take hold of what God is saying to you. I believe that there is a stirring on the inside of you to finish what God started in you. I labored in the spirit to write this book. This was a very difficult birthing process for me but worth every contraction that went into the finishing of it. I finished strong, now I am praying that you will allow the divine Seed of heaven to impregnate you with your purpose, destiny, and divine gifting and that you too will finish strong with what he gives you to give birth to for His Kingdom and Glory.

I hope this book has brought you understanding, motivation, and encouragement . At the beginning of hearing God's voice while putting this book together, as He spoke I wrote, I knew this would be a truly anointed manuscript for the body of Christ ; a message needed for people struggling with their purpose and destiny, and for those going through the long birthing process to get to God's Plan. I knew that there would be many hurting people who just wanted to give up. I knew there would be people who feel they just aren't good enough and who struggle with how people view them. I knew that God Almighty wanted to bring something so magnificent to their lives; something so powerful; and that, as they struggle with broken dreams, it would begin to nurture them, to build them up, to encourage them that it's not over. I knew that they would allow God to impregnate them with renewed faith, hope, and joy and they would see the dreams that God has for them come to pass.

Let's talk about your spiritual womb for a minute. Everywhere I go I see pregnant women. I can just go down to the convenience store or to get gas and I will see pregnant women. It seems like they're everywhere I go. My eyes will just lock on to the womb and how far along they are. For some, you can see that it's very new, and then for others they are walking around in agony and hoping that their water is going to break at any moment.

Some of you are like these different fruitful women I see; you are in different phases of your spiritual pregnancy. Maybe you are filled with passion and you're just in the dream stage right now. Some of you are farther along and you're not really in the dream stage anymore, and you have to close your eyes just to keep the dream alive. Some of you are at the stage where everything is about the purpose and the plan; the destiny and ministry that God has called you to. Others are in the place where they are so pregnant they just want to know when it's time to give birth. Some of you have been able to walk through the process to get to the promise. You are ready to truly walk in your divine purpose; what you were born for. You are ready to do what you were created to do; you know why you were put on this earth. There are different levels and different stages. Don't despise your time of preparation. Don't jump out ahead, and get in a hurry just wait on God.

> "Then the LORD answered me and said: "Write the vision and make it plain on tablets, That he may run who reads it. For the vision is yet for an appointed time; but at the end it will speak, and it will not lie. Though it tarries, wait for it; because it will surely come, It will not tarry." (Habakkuk 2:2, 3)

Submit yourself to the training, it is vitally important. I was a passionate, on fire for God, young man, and I'd try to shoot out ahead of God because I was full of zeal. I wanted to fulfill my purpose now. I received a prophecy and I was running with it, and that excites God. He put that on the inside of me because it helps me to be who I am and to do what I do.

We have to be careful, though, not to push out ahead of God. When you do that you can get out of the timing of God. When we do that, we run the risk of aborting, or miscarriage. We need to stay right in step and right in His timing. Just like a woman who is pregnant with her purpose, each phase, each month, trimester, and season of growth brings on different challenges and different feelings. In the beginning, you can't really tell a whole lot, because there's a lot of joy, excitement, and everybody is happy.

Praise God, you're pregnant! You're going to give birth; you're going to have a child. You go out looking for things, and buying things for the baby's room. That is the way it's supposed to be. Spiritually you need to run with your purpose when you give God the spiritual womb of your life. You purpose in your heart that you are going to do what God intended for you to do from the foundations of the world. Some of you are really excited and motivated and you're saying, I'm going to do this for God, and that for God, and that's good. You start dreaming, and thinking and planning. You do all the things that are just like a pregnant woman preparing for her child. After a while, you start getting excited and you fuel the anticipation. There's a baby coming, and life is changing. Life as you know it is never going to be the same.

Phaedra, B.J., and I were very comfortable, B.J. was on cruise control, and life was good. I was comfortable with how things were. Then, in just a matter of a year and a half, there they were. We had our new son, and then not long after that, we had our daughter Abigail. Just like that, we had two new children. Life as we knew it changed! In a moment my life was different and now everything is about the kid's schedules. Everything is centered on them; it has to be this way.

God has a scheduled plan for you too. When you least expect it; expect it, and then prepare for your life to change as you know it. Begin to dream big for yourself; dream big for God. There are no limitations to what God can do in and through you. God wants to use you, all it takes is one man or one woman to say yes to their purpose and destiny and it can change the course of a nation. See, this is not just about you or what you want. It's about the world and others around you ; it's about God making a huge investment inside you.

There's a huge investment inside of you. God gave His very best so that we could have the very best life. He loved you so much and He paid for it with His only begotten Son who died for you, and for me, and for the whole world. He's trying to redeem this world back to Himself. He's going to do it through you and me. Again, the Bible says, "The glory of the Lord shall cover the earth like the waters cover the sea." This will happen through us. We will push and gush Him out all over the world. The Father's water broke from heaven on this earth, and Jesus was born; a real Jesus that others could see and accept into their hearts and lives. Then transformation started coming to this world as we began to accept His divine purpose and destiny for our lives. The last instructions for each one of us, was given in Matthew 28:19-20 just before Jesus went up to be with the Father. He said, "Go therefore and make disciples of all the nations, baptizing them in the name of the Father, and of the Son, and of the Holy Spirit. Teaching them to observe all things that I have commanded you; and lo, I am with you always, even to the end of the age." We have a purpose and a destiny in that alone.

Maybe you're not totally sure what your purpose and destiny is, I just gave you one. The Bible gives us a mission, vision, and a purpose statement right there. Each and every one of us has a mission to win people to Jesus Christ however they can; to be a light unto this world. Remember, just like a baby doesn't start out fully grown in the womb, the same is true of your purpose and your destiny. Vision does not come into your life fully grown, it takes time to develop. God impregnates you, and the power of the Holy Spirit overshadows you, and He puts the seed of vision inside of you and births your purpose. In the Gospel of Luke, we see a powerful example of this very thing happening to Mary, the mother of Jesus. What a beautiful example of someone allowing God to impregnate them with the Seed of heaven and the Holy Spirit overshadowed Mary and impregnated not only her natural womb, but her heart and soul with the Seed of heaven; Jesus Christ, King of Kings, and Lord of Lords:

> "Now in the sixth month the angel Gabriel was sent by God to

> a city of Galilee called Nazareth, to a virgin betrothed to a man, whose name was Joseph, of the house of David. The virgin's name was Mary. And having come in, the angel said to her, "Rejoice, highly favored one, the Lord is with you; blessed are you among women!" But when she saw him, she was troubled at his saying, and considered what manner of greeting this was. Then the angel said to her, "Do not be afraid, Mary, for you have found favor with God. And behold, you will conceive in your womb, and bring forth a son, and shall call His name JESUS. He will be great, and will be called the Son of the highest; and the Lord God will give Him the throne of His father David. And He will reign over the house of Jacob forever, and of His kingdom, there will be no end. Then Mary said to the angel, "How can this be, since I do not know a man?" And the angel answered and said to her, "The Holy Spirit will come upon you, and the power of the Highest will overshadow you; therefore, also, that Holy One who is to be born will be called the Son of God." (Luke 1:26-35)

Doesn't that sum up everything we have covered? This is a mighty word from God that happened in both a physical and spiritual way and let me just tell you that Mary was a virgin. Don't allow the anti-Christ spirit to come and impregnate you, and invade the spiritual womb of your life. All across this country, right now, anti-Christ religions are rising up. Mindsets and thoughts are trying to infiltrate the church. They are trying to take away the Immaculate Conception. They are trying to say that Mary was not a virgin. If that's the case, it negates everything that we believe. Ministers, hold onto the truth, don't let it be taken away. We need to stand up for righteousness, because if we don't, no one is going to.

There are unrighteous judges in our country therefore, we need to be spiritual judges when it comes to the condition of our country and our world. We need to be Samson's; we need to be like the great judges of old;

there were evil judges, and there were also righteous judges . But it only took a few unrighteous judges to change the course of this nation. We need to begin to pray and interceded and stand up for righteousness sake once again in the United States.

Now, God, through His Spirit, wants to overshadow you, and impregnate you with His Son, Jesus, in the spiritual womb of your life. He wants to impregnate you just as He did Mary, with a purpose and a destiny. He wants you to give birth to the Son of the Living God, the Savior of the world, the Messiah. He wants to birth something in and through the spiritual womb of your life so that people can come to know the Savior of the world. He's the King of Kings and the Lord of Lords, He's Jesus.

Most of you may only remember Mary as the young girl who rode off on a donkey to facilitate the Christmas Story, but her life was so much more than that. It was a tapestry of mysteries that unraveled gradually throughout the seasons of her life, ultimately bringing her to her destiny at the foot of the cross. Mary was on a prophetic journey. She had been impregnated by the Seed of heaven and began to carry and walk out her purpose. She literally gave birth to the Savior of the world. This was the One who would restore and redeem mankind back to God the Father.

What an awesome and powerful ministry she had. Mary had a radical visitation from God. Can't you just hear her saying on that night so long ago, "The angel, Gabriel, came to me; I'm just a simple Jewish girl, living in poverty, in a little town called Nazareth." Can you imagine that? How many of you, when the Lord came to you and said He wanted to do something in and through you said, "I'm just a guy from Arizona" (or wherever it was that you were born). Maybe you are saying, "How can God use a young Amish man like me?"

We had a man in our church body that came from the Amish community, named David Wickey. He had the beard, the hat, and the buggy. One day the Lord spoke to him that He was going to use him to be a deliverer to these people, calling Him back to the Amish community, and he said, "Who am I?" I'm just like Moses, "I can't speak" and God said, "I'm going to use a stutterer to be a deliverer to My people and to bring My children out from the land of bondage and into the Promised Land.

Moses needed a burning bush. What do you need? You don't need a burning bush because you have a fire on the inside of you. You don't need a sign because everything you need has been provided for in Christ. Jesus Christ dwells and lives in us. The Bible says, "It is Christ within us; the hope of glory."

Remember, the angel said, "Rejoice, highly favored one, the Lord is with you; blessed are you among women!" He told her not to fear and that she would give birth to the Messiah, and she cried out, "Yes, Lord, let it be done unto me according to your word." What an answer. I believe if we could flash back to that very moment in time in history and see a picture on the wall of what happened, I believe that we would see that it was at the very moment she said, "Yes, Lord" that the shadow of the Spirit came in and overshadowed her. He impregnated her with the Seed of heaven. He's the One that was, and is, and is to come. He's the One in the beginning who made all things and nothing that was made was made without Him. The Holy Spirit came, overshadowed her, and impregnated her inside her physical womb. Mary was a sovereign vessel chosen to be the mother of Jesus.

The Bible does not indicate that she moved in miracles. She was not Deity material, like other religions tried to make her. Nowhere in God's Holy Word do we find that Mary would be elevated to god-like status. Nowhere do we find anyone else or any other mediator who could get us to Jesus. "For there is one God, and one mediator between God and man, the man Christ Jesus." (I Timothy 2:5) Mary simply had a heart of devotion and a child-like faith unlike any other woman of her day. She had a willingness like none other to become pregnant with promise. When she said, "Yes, Lord, let it be done unto me according to your word...," it changed her life forever.

We can all have a holy respect for Mary, and want to be like her because when she was asked, she said, "Yes, Lord," that is a true example to follow. This is your moment to say "Yes!" It's your moment to say yes to your purpose and destiny. It is your moment to say yes to your future. Everything you've done to this point has prepared you for where you're going and brought you to this moment of your life. All of your heartaches, hurts, pain, disappointments, and sorrow, all of your faults, and failures, have led you to this day to say, "Yes, Lord! I say yes to my purpose and yes to my destiny in You. I say yes to my opportunities, yes, Lord, yes!"

The Lord looked across the face of the earth and said, "Who will go for me?" One man named Isaiah said, "Here I am, Lord, send me. I will go for you." Then He took from the fire the coals from off of the altar and put it on his lips. It's now time for you to say, "Yes, Lord; here I am send me!" God wants to give you His holy fire from the coals of His altar and anoint you for destiny. Some of you have been going for many years and it is time for you to get the holy fire of God inside you that will burn passionately within you.

For ten years I had consistent turmoil in my life, but I had to understand and know what it was like to carry and give birth to the purpose and destiny on the inside of me. Maybe your true purpose and destiny is still in your spiritual womb and it's taking longer than you thought it would, that's okay. There is a divine destiny, appointment, and timing for the purpose of God. This is the moment for you to push into your purpose and destiny. It's time to say "Yes, Lord!" Are you ready? There are those who hear the truth, but they're not ready to receive it. Are you ready to give birth? Mary had the courage to say yes, it was her prophetic destiny. We have to believe that God impregnated us with vision and purpose. We have to believe Him and know that this is what He wants us to do. If you waiver, you will run the risk of spiritual miscarriage.

In the Bible there was a man who needed healing for his child and the Lord asked him, "Do you believe?" And his next statement was, "Lord, I believe, but help my unbelief." Some of you are right there, you want to believe it and you really want to see God's purpose and destiny for your life. You really want to give birth to those things, but you're struggling. Ask Him and say as this man did, "Lord, I believe but help my unbelief." It was said of Mary; "Blessed is she who believed, for there will be a fulfillment of those things which were told to her of the Lord.." If you believe in your heart and do not doubt there will be a fulfillment of those things which were told to you from the Lord!

There are words over my church, my Bible college, and my personal calling that I'm just now starting to see come to pass after many years of waiting. There are words over my wife and I that we are just now beginning to see in their fullness after many years of laboring in ministry. There are promises over your life too and there will be a fulfillment of those things which were told to you from the Lord but the key is that you have to believe!

The enemy will try to come in and he will lie to you. He wants to make you believe that none of this is real. He will come to your thoughts and say, "You have just been living a dream, this was never God. What were you thinking? Have you lost your mind or something? Who are you to think you hear from God anyway?" He started it in the Garden of Eden and he is still doing it today. As soon as the devil got wind of what the Holy Spirit had done in Mary, he moved on some unrighteous judge and had all the babies in his region killed. The same thing happened to Moses. The enemy had stepped in to take God's babies just as he is still doing today by the millions. Moses' mother said, "Lord, I'll do what you ask to protect this child."

Sometimes the Lord may ask you to do some pretty painful things so that a destiny can be fulfilled in the earth. Some of you are holding onto things so tightly that God can't even get close enough to you to impregnate you, to birth something in you, and bless you. You are holding on so tightly you can't sleep at night. God is saying to let go and hold on to Him.

Think about the heartache of what Moses' mother had to do. She put him to her breast one last time and then she let him go. Immediately Pharaoh's wife asked that someone be found to feed this child. Can you imagine? She had to go through the repeated daily routine of taking her son up to her breast and then sending him back. Only mothers know the bond that forms at that time. Yet, she had to release Moses over and over again into the care of Pharaoh's home. She knew he wasn't being taught in the manner she would have taught him, and she knew that the Egyptians believed in false gods. Yet, she did what God asked her to do. Mothers, you know many of you would have held on and said, "No, God, don't ask me to send him back again. Why, God, why? Can't you just use your power to keep him safe here in my home?"

God had made His plan clear. We can't hold on, we have to completely let our dream die, just as Pastor Phaedra had to let hers die. I had to let my ministry, in the middle of great success, go. I had to let it die, and it did. God took care of Moses and put him in Pharaoh's house. It's amazing that the very one who would say to Pharaoh, "Let my people go." was being raised up right under his own roof.

There are still a few of you out there who just won't let go. You have convinced yourself that it will change even though it is still in your hands. You are putting all your faith, hope, and trust in your strength. Why? It's His purpose, and the Lord is saying, "let it go." It's not your way, it's His way. The thing that you're holding on to is not your security blanket. Let it go! As Moses' mother placed him in the basket and put it in the water, she didn't know where it would lead him. It took being obedient to God, and trusting Him. God the Father let His son go, so He knows what you're feeling. He knows what it takes, the sacrifices, and the anguish in releasing something so close to your heart. If you let go, the Lord will take your situation and transform it; let it go and watch what He will do."

> "My soul magnifies the Lord, and my spirit has rejoiced in God my Savior. For He has regarded the lowly state of His maid-servant; for behold, henceforth, all generations will call me blessed. For He who is mighty has done great things for me, and Holy is His name." (Luke 1:46-49)

Think about it, Mary's life was used to help usher in revival and transformation in her day. Do you want your life to usher in revival in your day? Open up your mouth right now and say, "Lord, let it be done unto me according to your Word. Lord, I want to be like Mary; overshadow me by the power of your Holy Spirit. Impregnate me with your purposes." Are you willing to be a carrier of purpose and destiny? Are you willing to bring the glory of God to your family, to your workplace, your neighborhood, to the church, and to the world? Are you ready to take this to your generation? Then open up your heart, your spiritual womb, and let the divine Seed of heaven in. Let His Holy Spirit overshadow you and impregnate you with your purpose and destiny, and then with everything within you push and you too will see, know, and fulfill your true purpose and destiny in the earth!